Arlo Bates

A Book of Nine Tales

Arlo Bates

A Book of Nine Tales

ISBN/EAN: 9783337023638

Printed in Europe, USA, Canada, Australia, Japan

Cover: Foto ©Andreas Hilbeck / pixelio.de

More available books at **www.hansebooks.com**

A

BOOK O' NINE TALES

ARLO BATES

BOSTON
ROBERTS BROTHERS
1891

University Press:

JOHN WILSON AND SON, CAMBRIDGE, U.S.A.

To my Friend

HERBERT HARRIS.

CONTENTS.

Tale the First.

---•---

A STRANGE IDYL.

A BOOK O' NINE TALES.

A STRANGE IDYL.

I.

E lay upon an old-fashioned bedstead whose carved quaintness would once have pleased him, but to which he was now indifferent. He rested upon his back, staring at the ceiling, on whose white surface were twinkling golden dots and lines in a network which even his broken mind knew must be the sunlight reflected from off the water somewhere. The windows of the chamber were open, and the sweet summer air came in laden with the perfume of flowers piquantly mingled with pungent sea odors. Now and then a bee buzzed by the casement, or a butterfly seemed tempted to enter the sick-room — apparently thought better of it, and went on its careless way.

Of all these things the sick man who lay there was unconscious, and the sweet young

girl sitting by his bed was too deeply buried
in her book to notice them.   For some time
there was no movement in the chamber, until,
the close of a chapter releasing for an instant
the reader's attention, she looked to discover
that the patient's eyes were open.   Seeing
him awake, she rose and came a step nearer,
thereby making the second discovery, more
startling than the first, that the light of reason had replaced in those eyes the stare of
delirium.

"Ah," she said, softly, "you are awake!"

The invalid turned his gaze toward her, far
too feeble to make any other movement ; but
he made no attempt to speak.

"No," she continued, with that little purr-
ing intonation which betrays the feminine
satisfaction at having a man helpless and unable to resist coddling ; "don't speak.   Take
your medicine, and go to sleep again."

She put a firm, round arm beneath his
head, and bestowed upon him a spoonful of
a colorless liquid, afterward smoothing his pillows with deft, swift touches.   He submitted
with utter passiveness of mind and body, ignorant who this maiden might be, where he
was, or, indeed, who he was.   Painfully he
endeavored to think, to remember, to understand ; but with no result save confusing

himself and bringing on an ache in his head. His nurse, at the convenient end of another chapter, observed a look of pain and trouble upon the thin face, scarcely less white than the pillow against which it rested.

"You are worrying," she observed with authority. "Go to sleep. You are not to think yet."

And, staying himself upon the resolution and confidence in her tone, he abandoned himself again to the current of circumstances, and drifted away into dreams.

The girl, watching closely now, with mind distracted from her story to the more tangible mystery involved in the presence of the sick man, gave a little sigh of relief when his even breathing indicated that he had fallen asleep. She removed softly to a seat near the window, and looked out upon the tranquil beauty of the afternoon. Long Island Sound lay before her, dimpling and twinkling in the sunshine, while nearer a sloping lawn stretched from the house to the shore. Glancing backward and forward between the sunny landscape and the bed where her patient slept, the maiden fell to wondering about him, recalling the little she knew, and straining her fancy to construct the story of his life.

Three weeks before a Sound steamer had been wrecked so near this spot that through the stormy night she had seen the glare of the fire which broke out before the hull sank, and the next morning's tide had brought to shore this man, a floating waif, saved by a life-preserver and some propitious current. A terrible wound upon his head showed where he had experienced some blow, and left him hesitating with distraught brain between life and death. In his delirium he had muttered of varied scenes. He must, the watcher reflected, have travelled extensively. Now there were words which showed that he was sharing in wild escapades; cries of defiance or of encouragement to comrades whose shadowy forms his disordered brain summoned from the mysterious past ; strange names, and words in unknown tongues mingled themselves with incoherent appeals or bitter reproaches.

To the girl who had been scarcely less at his bedside than the old woman who nominally nursed him, these broken fragments of wild talk had been like bits of jewels from which her mind had fashioned a fantastic mosaic. The mystery surrounding the stranger would, in any case, have appealed strongly to her quick fancy, but when

to this was added the brilliancy of his deliri-
ous ravings, it is small wonder that her imagination took fire, and she wove endless ro-
mances, in all of which the unconscious sick
man figured as the hero. Scraps of talk in
an unknown tongue, a few sonorous foreign
words, a little ignorance concerning matters
in reality commonplace enough, have, in
many a case before, been the sufficient foun-
dations for a gorgeous *fata morgana* of fancy.

The stranger had been thrown ashore only
partially dressed, and with nothing upon him
which bore a name. A belt around his waist
contained about fifteen hundred dollars in
bills and a small quantity of gold-dust. From
the presence of this latter they had specu-
lated that the wounded man might be a returning Californian, yet his clothing was of
too fine texture and manufacture for this supposition. Several persons, seeking for friends
lost in the disaster from which he came, had
vainly endeavored to identify him, and his
description had been given in the New York
papers; but without result. There seemed,
upon the whole, to be no especial hope of
obtaining any satisfactory information regarding the sick man until he was able to furnish
it himself; and to-day for the first time the
watcher found in his eyes the light of return-

ing reason. She felt as if upon the threshold
of a great discovery. She smiled softly to
herself to think how eager she had become
over this mystery; to recognize how large a
place the stranger occupied in her thoughts;
yet she could but acknowledge to herself that
this was an inevitable consequence of the
existence which surrounded her.

The life into which the wounded man had
been driven by the currents of the sea and
those stronger currents of the universe which
we call Fate was a sufficiently monotonous
one. The household into which he had
been received consisted of an old gentleman,
broken alike in health and fortune, so that
while the establishment over which presided
his only child was not one of absolute want,
it was often straitened by the necessity of
uncomfortable economies. Alone with an
old family servant, the father and daughter
lived on in the homestead which the wealth
of their ancestors had improved, but which
their present revenues were inadequate to
preserve in proper state. One day with them
was so like every other day that the differences of the calendar seemed purely empir-
ical, even when assisted by such diversity as
old Sarah, the faithful retainer, was able to
compass in the matter of the viands which,

at stated periods in the week, appeared upon their frugal table.

Old Mr. Dysart would have failed to perceive the justice of the epithet "selfish" as applied to himself ; yet no word so perfectly described him. He was absorbed in the compilation of a complete genealogy of the entire Dysart family, with all its ramifications and allied branches. What became of his daughter while he delved among musty parchments in his stately old library; how the burdens of the household were borne ; and how a narrow income was made to cover expenses, were plainly matters upon which he could not be expected to waste his valuable time. The maiden could scarcely have been more alone upon a desert island, or in a magic tower. Her days followed each other with slow, monotonous flow, like the sands in an hour-glass, — each like the one before, and each, too, like the one to follow.

Amid such a colorless waste of existence the rich mystery of the wounded stranger appeared doubly brilliant by contrast ; and it is small wonder that to the watcher the first gleam of returning intelligence in the sick man's eyes was as the promise of the opening of a door behind which lay an enchanted palace.

II.

IT was yet a day or two before the sick man spoke. He was very weak, and lay for the most part in a deathlike but health-giving sleep. At length the day came when he said feebly : —

" Where am I ? "

" Here." his nurse answered, with truly feminine irrelevancy.

" Where ? "

" At Glencarleon."

He lay silent for some moments, evidently struggling to attach some meaning to the name, and to collect his strength for further inquiries.

His eyes expressed his mental confusion.

" You were hurt in the steamer accident," she explained. " You came ashore here, and are with friends. Don't try to talk. It is all right."

He was too feeble to remonstrate, — too feeble even to reason, and he obeyed her injunction of silence without protest. She retreated to her favorite seat by the window, and took up her sewing ; but her revery progressed more rapidly than her stitches,

and when she was relieved from her post by
old Sarah, she stole softly out of the room
to continue her dreaming in an arbor over-
looking the water, where, in pleasant weather,
she was wont to spend her leisure hours.

The next day, when she gave her patient
his morning gruel, he watched her with questioning eyes, as if endeavoring to identify
her, and at last framed another inquiry.

" Who are you ? " he asked.

" I am Columbine."

" Columbine ? "

" Columbine Dysart."

That he knew little more than before was
a consequence of the situation, and Mistress
Columbine was wise enough to spare him the
necessity of saying so.

" You do not know us," she said ; " but we
will take good care of you until you are well
enough to hear all about it."

" But — " he began, the puzzled look upon
his wan face not at all dissipated.

" No," she returned, " there is no ' but '
about it. It is all right."

" But," he repeated with an insistence that
would not be denied, " but — "

" Well ? " queried she, seeing that something
troubled him too much to be evaded.

" But who am I ? " he demanded, so earnestly that the absurdity of such a question was lost in its pathos.

"Who are you?" she echoed, in bewilderment. Then, with the instant reflection that he was still too near delirium and brain-fever to be allowed to trouble himself with speculations, she added, brightly, and with the air of one who settles all possible doubts, "Why, you are yourself, of course."

She smiled so dazzlingly as she spoke that a complete faith in her assurances mingled itself with some dimly felt sense of the ludicrous in the sick man's mind, and although the baffled look did not at once disappear from his face, yet he said nothing further, and not long after he fell asleep, leaving Columbine free to seek her arbor again and ponder on this new phase of her interesting case. She attached no serious importance then to the fact that her patient seemed so uncertain concerning his identity; but, as the days went by, and he was as completely unable to answer his own query as ever, a strange, baffled feeling stole over her; a teasing sense of being brought helplessly face to face with a mystery to which she had no key.

His convalescence was somewhat slow, the hurts he had received having been of a very serious nature; but when he was able to leave his room, and even to accompany Columbine to her favorite arbor, he was still grappling vainly with the problem of who and what he was.

This first visit to 'the arbor, it should be noted, was an event in the quiet life at the old house. Columbine was full of petty excitement over it, her fair cheeks flushed and her hair disordered with running to and fro to see that the cushions were in place, the sun shining at the right angle, and the breeze not too fresh. She insisted upon supporting the sick man on one side, while faithful old Sarah, her nurse in childhood, and since promoted to fill at once the place of house-keeper and all the departed servants, took his arm upon the other to help him along the smoothly trodden path through the neglected garden. Mr. Dysart was as usual in his library, and to disturb him there was a venture requiring more daring than either of the women possessed. They got on very tolerably without him, however, and the patient was soon installed amid a pile of wraps and shawls in the summer-house, where he was left in charge of Miss Dysart, while Sarah returned to her household avocations.

It was a beautiful day in the beginning of September, warm and golden, with all the mellowness of autumn in the air, while yet the glow of summer was not wholly lost. The soft sound of water on the shore was heard through the chirping of innumerable insects, shrilling out their delight in the heat; while now and then the notes of a bird mingled pleasantly in the harmony. The convalescent drew in full breaths of the sweet air with a sigh of satisfaction, leaning back among his cushions to look, with the pleasure of returning life, over the fair scene before him.

For some time nurse and patient sat silent, but the girl, watching him intently, was in no wise dissatisfied with the other's evident appreciation of her favorite spot. Indeed, she had dreamed here of him so often that some subtle, clairvoyancy may have secretly put him in harmony with the place before he saw it. Columbine liked him for the pleasure so evident upon his handsome, wasted face, while inly she was aware how great would have been her disappointment had he been less alive to the charms of the view.

" How lovely it is ! " he said, at length. " It is, perhaps, because you live in so lovely a place," he added, after a trifling pause, and with a faint smile, " that you are so kind to a waif like myself."

" Perhaps," she answered, returning his smile. "But, really, we only did what any one would have done in our place."

" Oh, no; and besides, few could have done it so well. It is so pleasant, I seem to have lived here always."

"It may be," Columbine suggested, with deliberation, "that it recalls some place you have known."

A shadow came over his face.

"It is a pity," he said, "that if that un-lucky disaster could spare me nothing of my baggage, it could not at least have left me my few poor wits. I might make an interesting case for psychologists. They might discover from me in what part of the brain the faculty of memory is located, for that wretched wound seems to have let mine all ooze out of my cranium. I do not feel, Miss Dysart, like an idiot in all respects, since I certainly know my right hand from my left ; and I have found, by experiment in the night-watches, that I could still make myself understood in two or three languages."

"You had much better have slept," inter-polated his listener.

"But as far as my personal history goes," he continued, replying to her words by a smile, " my mind is an absolute blank. I can give you several interesting pieces of information concerning ancient history and chronology; but I have n't the faintest idea what my name is; and you must acknowledge that it is a little hard for a man to be ignorant of his own name."

" Yes," Columbine assented, bending forward and clasping her hands in front of her knees. " Yes; and it is so strange! Try and remember; you must surely recollect something."

" I have tried; I do try; but I can only conjure up a confused mass of shifting images; things I seem to have been and to have done, all indistinguishably mixed with what I have only dreamed or hoped to do and be."

" How strange! " she said again, fixing her wide-open dark eyes upon him, and then turning her gaze to the sea beyond; " but it will come to you in time."

" Heavens! " he exclaimed, energetically, " I hope so, else I shall regret that you pulled me out of the water. To-day I do seem to have a glimpse of something more tangible. Since I sat here I almost thought I remembered —"

He broke off suddenly, his bright look fading into an expression of helpless annoyance.

" What? " cried Columbine, eagerly.

"I cannot tell," he groaned. "It is all gone."

"Oh, what a pity!" exclaimed she, springing to her feet in a flush of sympathy and baffled curiosity. "Oh, how cruel!"

Then she remembered that she was absolutely disobeying the doctor's orders, and was allowing her patient to become excited.

"There, there," she said, "how wrong of me to let you worry! Everything will come back to you when you are stronger. Now it is time for your luncheon. It is so warm and bright you may have it here if you will promise not to bother your head. For I really think," she added, wisely, giving his wraps a deft touch or two, "that the best way to remember is not to try."

"I dare say you are right," he agreed. "At least trying does n't seem to accomplish much."

She flitted away, to return a moment or two later with an old-fashioned salver, upon which, in dainty china two or three generations old, Sarah had arranged the invalid's luncheon. She drew the rustic table up to his side and served him, while he ate with that mixture of eagerness and disinclination which marks the appetite of one in the early stages of a convalescence.

"That pitcher," he observed, carelessly, as she poured out the cream, "ought to belong to my past. It has a familiar look, as if it could claim acquaintance if it would only deign."

"It was my grandmother's," Columbine said. "When we were little, Cousin Tom used to tease me by saying my cheeks looked like those of that fat face on the handle. I was more buxom then than now."

Instead of replying, her companion laid down his spoon and looked at her in delighted amaze. Then he struck his hands together with sudden vigor.

"Tom!" he cried. "Tom!"

"Well?" queried she, looking at him as if he had gone distraught. "It isn't so strange a name, is it?"

"But, don't you see?" he exclaimed, joyously, — "I'm Tom! I have found my name!"

III.

THE rest of Tom's name, however, remained as profoundly and as provokingly concealed in the wounded convolutions of his brain as ever. Columbine called him Mr. Tom, and it is not unlikely that the famil-

iarity of the monosyllable, which seemed to
place them at once upon an intimate footing,
had a strong influence upon their relations.
The maiden had a crisp way of pronouncing
the name, as if she were half conscious of a
spice of impropriety in a term so familiar,
and felt it, too, to be something of a joke,
which was so wholly fascinating that the patient did not have to be very far advanced
toward his normal condition of health and
spirits to enjoy it so well as to reflect that
the name so rendered ought to be enough
for any man.

Mr. Tom soon began to gather up a few
stray bits from his childhood, his memory
apparently returning to its former state by
the same slow road it had travelled from his
birth to reach it.

"I remember a few beginnings," he had
said, hopefully, on the day following that of
his first visit to the arbor. "I had a carved
coral of a most luscious pink color. It is
even now vaguely connected in my mind
with the idea of eating; so I infer that I
must have cherished a fond delusion that it
was good to eat."

"It is at least good to remember," Columbine returned, laughing. "It wouldn't be a
bad idea to open an account of things re-

covered from the sea of the past. You can
begin by putting down: Item, one coral."

. "Yes; and one nurse. I distinctly recall
the nurse. She had a large mole on her
chin. Yes; I can certainly swear to the
nurse."

He was in excellent spirits to-day. The
dawning of recollection gave promise of
the restoration of complete remembrance;
the day was enchanting; his appetite and his
luncheon came to a wonderfully good agree-
ment, while a prettier serving-maid than Miss
Dysart could hardly be found.

"It must be very like being a child again,"
she observed, thoughtfully; "and that is a
thing, you know, for which the poets are
always sighing."

"You will have the advantage of growing
up with me," was his gay retort, "if this
process continues. Only you'll have the advantage of superior age."

After that he told her each morning what
he had been able to recover from forgetful-
ness since the previous day. It is difficult
to imagine the strangeness of this relation.
It possessed all the piquancy of fiction to
which its ingenious author added new incidents from day to day; yet it had, too, the
strong attractiveness of truth and personal

interest. Columbine listened and commented, deeply engrossed and fascinated by the novel experience which gave her an acquaintance with the entire past life of her stranger guest, yet an acquaintance which was etherealized and marked by a certain charm not to be found in actual companionship. Had she really shared the childhood thus narrated to her it would have been in no way remarkable; but now she seemed to live it herself, with a vitality and interest more vivid each day. Often the freakish faculty, upon whose vigor depended the continuity of Mr. Tom's narration, would for days concern itself with the veriest trifles, advancing the essentials of the story not a whit; or, again, it would seem to turn perversely backward, although no efforts availed to speed it forward.

The main facts of Mr. Tom's story, so far as they were gathered up in the first week of this odd story-telling, were as follows: He made his acquaintance with the world doubly orphaned, his father being lost at sea upon a return voyage from India before the boy's birth, and his ·mother dying in childbed. Reflecting upon what he was able to recall, Tom concluded that his parents were persons of wealth. His surroundings had at least been luxurious. The truth was, as he came,

in time, to remember, that, being left without
near relatives, he had been, by his guardian,
confided to the care of trusty people, who
spoiled and adored him until he was trans-
ferred to boarding-school.

"I have grown to be a dozen years old,"
Tom remarked to Miss Dysart one afternoon
as they sat in the arbor, she sewing, and he
idly pulling to pieces a purple aster. "I
have even conducted myself to boarding-
school, and I cannot conceive why I can't
get hold of my family name. I must have
been called by it sometimes. I remember
being dubbed Tom, Tommy, Thomas, — that
was when I was stubborn; Tom Titmouse —
that was by nurse; Tom Tattamus — that by
the particularly odious small boy next door;
but beyond that I might as well never have
had a name at all. My trunks, I know, were
marked with a big W, but all the names beginning with that letter that I can hit upon
seem equally strange to me. I do not see
why, of all things, it is precisely that which
I cannot remember."

"It is because you worry about it," his
companion suggested; "probably that particular spot in your brain where your name
is lodged is kept irritated by your impatience."

"Heavens!" laughed he. "How psychologic and physiological you are! Well, if I've no name, I can invent one, I suppose."

"Or make one. Do you realize what a fascinating position you are in? Common mortals have only the consolation of speculating about their future; but you can also amuse yourself with boundless speculations concerning your past. You are relieved from all responsibility —"

"Oh, no," he interrupted; "that is the worst of it. I have responsibilities without knowing what they are. The past holds me like a giant from behind, and I cannot even see my captor."

"Oh, you look at it all too seriously!" Columbine returned. "You can fashion your past, as we all do our futures, just as you like. I think you are decidedly to be envied."

"Envied!"

The bitterness of the exclamation brought to her a sudden realization of the difference of their points of view, and revealed how deep was the man's humiliation at his helpless position. A quick flush of pity and sympathy mantled her cheek.

"Forgive me," she exclaimed, impulsively. "I had no right to be so thoughtless. I beg your pardon."

" There is no occasion. You are right. It
is certainly better to laugh than to cry over
the inevitable, especially as things are right-
ing themselves. But we, or, rather, I, must
go into the house. It is growing cool."

IV.

LIFE at the old Dysart place went forward
in a slow and decorous fashion, little allied
to the bustling manners of the present day.
Mr. Dysart was getting now to be an old
man, albeit it is doubtful if in any abundant
sense he can ever have been a young one.
In any case he had, by long burrowing among
musty records and genealogical parchments,
acquired a dry and antique appearance, as,
to use a somewhat presumptuous yet not in-
exact metaphor, certain scholarly worms had
taken on a brown hue from continued dining
on the bindings of his venerable folios. He
inhabited a remote and essentially unworldly
sphere, from which the existence of his
daughter was wholly separate. He was conscious of her presence in an unrealizing
way; was even aware that just now she had
in the house a guest who had come ashore
from a wreck. But that was the affair of

Columbine and old Sarah; he could not of course be expected to loosen his hold upon the clew which he hoped would lead him to the exact connection between the Dysarts and the Van Rensselaers of two generations back, to pay attention to a chance waif from that outer world with which he had never considered it worth his while to concern himself.

As far as Mr. Tom was concerned, Mr. Dysart might as well not have existed. They did once meet in the passage before the study door when the invalid in his first days of walking was one rainy morning wandering restlessly about the halls; but the owner of the house hurried furtively past, as if he were the interloper and the other lord of the manor; and even when the convalescent was well enough to join the family at table, Mr. Dysart was very seldom there, so that the meals were for the most part taken *tête-à-tête* by Columbine and her patient.

The result of such a situation is evident from the beginning. Exceptional natures might be imagined, perhaps, that would not have grown dangerously interested in each other under such circumstances; but at least these two drew every day closer together. Neither had any tie belonging to the past;

or, more exactly, Columbine had none, and
he, for the time being, at least, had no past.
His helplessness and the mystery enshroud-
ing him would have appealed to the heart of
any woman, and Columbine had no distrac-
tions to fill her life and crowd out this ever-
deepening interest. Of Mr. Tom, her beauty
and freshness, her simplicity, which was so
far removed from insipidity, her innocence,
which never suggested ignorance, won the re-
spect and admiration long before he was conscious that love, too, was growing in his heart.

There came a day, however, when he could
no longer be ignorant of the nature of his
feelings.

The two had gone past the arbor and down
to the shore. Columbine was seated upon a
rock, while Tom lay at her feet, idly tossing
pebbles into a pool left among the sea-weed
by the ebbing tide. The maiden wore that
day a dress of gray flannel, almost the color
of the stone upon which she sat, trimmed
with a velvet of orange which no complexion
less brilliant than hers could have endured.
She twisted in her fingers a spray of golden-
rod, yellow-coated harbinger of autumn.

"The summer is gone," Columbine remarked, pensively. "It is getting late even
for golden-rod."

"Yes," he echoed, "the summer is gone. I lost so much of it I hardly realize —"

He broke off suddenly, a new thought seizing him.

"Why!" he exclaimed, "how long I have been here! I ought to have taken myself off your hands long ago. How you must think I abuse your hospitality!" .

"Nonsense!" she returned, brightly; "you of course cannot go until you are well. It is necessary that you at least conjure from the past the rest of your name before you start out into the world again. Make yourself as comfortable as you can, Mr. Tom; you won't be let loose for a long time to come yet."

Despite the lightness of her manner her companion fancied he detected a shade of some hitherto unnoted feeling in her words; but whether dread of his departure or desire to be rid of him he could not divine. The latter thought struck him with a sudden chill. The love which had been fostered in his mind by this close and intimate companionship was not unmixed at this moment with a fear of being thrown upon his own resources while ignorant alike of his place and his name. He clung strongly to Columbine as to one who understood and sympathized with his strange

3

mental weakness.   The color flamed into his
pale cheeks with a sudden throb of intense
emotion; then faded, to leave him whiter
than ever.

" Besides," Columbine continued, after a
moment's pause, her glance still downcast,
" why should n't you stay?   Your being here
makes no difference to papa; he smokes and
grubs after the roots of his ancestral tree the
same as ever; and as for me," lifting her
eyes with a sudden smile that showed all her
dimples, " you know how much you amuse
me.   You are as good as a continued story,
and are alive, too, the last being a good
deal in this desert."

He returned her smile with effort.   His
moment of intense feeling had so overpow-
ered him that he felt weak and faint.

" How white you are !" she exclaimed,
noting the wanness of his face; " you should
have had your *bouillon* long ago.   A pretty
condition you are in to go roaming off by
yourself ! "

She tripped lightly off towards the house
for the forgotten nourishment, and Mr. Tom
was left to his reflections.   He raised himself,
as her graceful figure vanished, then sank
back upon his rug with something like a
groan.   All in an instant the knowledge had

come to him that he loved her. He had gone on from day to day conscious only of thinking of his own history, which, bit by bit, he was disinterring from the past, as men bring to light some buried city, and insensibly Columbine had become dear to him before he was aware.

He buried his face in his hands in a despair which was in part the result of his strange mental confusion; in part arose from his physical weakness. He did not reflect then that his case was not necessarily hopeless; that nothing in his life which remembrance had recovered need raise a barrier between himself and Columbine. Afterward this thought came to him and brought comfort; now he was overwhelmed by a sense of impotent misery. Helpless in the hand of fate, it seemed to him that this love, of which he was newly aware, was but a fresh device of malignant destiny. He did not even consider whether his affection might be returned; he only felt the impossibility of offering his broken life to Columbine, — of binding her to a past that was uncertain and a future that was insecure.

Tears of weakness, and scorn of that weakness, came into his eyes. Their traces were still visible when Columbine returned.

"Come," she said, ignoring the signs of

his agitation, " you have told me nothing on
the story to-day.   Just down there," indicat-
ing by a pretty sweep of the hand a little
pebbly cove lying just below them, " is where
Sarah and I found you."

"And I would to God," cried poor Tom
with sudden fierceness, "that you had left me
there."

Columbine made, for the moment, no reply
to this outburst.   She insisted upon his drink-
ing his *bouillon*, despite his protests of disinclination, and then brought him back to the
tale of his life.

"There is an air of improbability about
my story," he said, after a little musing.
"Indeed, so much so that I myself begin to
doubt the truth of it.   In the first place it
seems particularly arranged to baffle inquiry.
Whenever I recall a person to whom I might
send for verification or information, I straight-
way remember that he is dead, or that my
wanderings have carried me beyond his
knowledge.   I am apparently as far as ever
from knowing who I am or what I am.   And,
besides, suppose your beautiful theory, that
my memory acts as it does because the impressions of youth are strongest, is not true?
You put me in the same category with those
whose memory is weakened by age; but this

may be all moonshine. Perhaps this history, to which I am painfully adding every day, is something I have read, and only a fiction after all."

"But why suppose so many tormenting things?" returned Columbine, brightly. "The fault of the age, they say, — we know very little of it here, but cousin Tom sends me a paper occasionally, — is unrest; and whoever you are, a little tranquillity will scarcely be likely to harm you. Go on with the life and adventures, and never mind now whether they are true or not. At least they are interesting. You broke off yesterday in a most exciting account of a tiger hunt."

"Ah, yes; I got the rest of it together this morning. Where did I leave off? Had we reached the second jungle?"

V.

THE salt meadows were on fire. The pungent odor of burning peat and saline grasses floated over the Dysart place and about the arbor one October morning when Tom sat there meditating. He was thinking of Columbine, and of his passion for her. His health now seemed firmly re-establishing itself, and his memory had gone on over the

old track of his life in its singular method of
progression until he felt confident that he
should ultimately be in possession of all his
past. He reviewed what he remembered, as
he sat this morning inhaling the aromatic
scent of the burning lowlands, and the result
was not unsatisfactory. He had recovered
from oblivion his life up to the time, three
years before, when he took passage home
from India, and his financial affairs at that
period were in an eminently satisfactory position. He recalled that he had been regarded
on shipboard as a person of more consequence than the British officer who, with his
daughter, occupied the cabin of the India-
man with him; and he trusted that no un-
toward circumstances of the interval had
placed him in a condition less desirable.

He had reconciled himself to remaining at
the Dysart mansion by turning over to old
Sarah a goodly portion of the money contained in his travelling-belt, and blessed himself that his wandering life had led him to
form the habit of always going thus provided.
He sat now waiting for Columbine to appear,
and fondly picturing to himself the delight
of telling his love when the time came that he
dare speak. Each day increased his attachment, and he believed, as every lover will,

that his love was returned. A smile of brooding contentment, so deep that even the impatience of his passion could not disturb it, dwelt upon his face as he inhaled the fragrant odors from the burning marshes, and listened for the step of the maiden he loved.

She came at last, moving along the garden paths between the faded shrubs, a gracious and winning figure. She was dressed that morning in a gown of russet wool, with a bunch of gold and crimson leaves at her throat, and never, in Tom's eyes, had she looked so lovely.

" I should n't have been so late in getting here," she said, as she took her accustomed seat, " but Sarah is greatly concerned about the fire in the salt marshes. She says it is thirty years since they burnt over, and she presages all sorts of dire calamities from that fact."

" That they have n't burnt over for thirty years? "

" Well," Columbine returned with a pout, " she is not at all clear what she does mean, so it is n't to be expected that I shall be. We will go on with the life and adventures, if you please."

" But suppose I have n't remembered anything more? "

"Nonsense," retorted pretty Columbine; "you never really remember. I am convinced that you make it all up as you go along; but you tell it so seriously that it might as well be true. And in any case it does credit to your powers of imagination."

His story now was of his voyage from Calcutta. He told of moonlight nights in the Indian ocean, of long days of sunny idling on deck, and all the pleasant details of a prosperous voyage over Southern seas.

"Miss Grant wasn't very pretty," he observed, lying lazily back and looking up into the blue October sky, "at least not as I remember her; but she was very good company, only a little given to sentimentalizing. She had a guitar, and I will confess I did hate to see that guitar come out."

"She would be pleased if she could hear you," laughed Columbine. "What was there so frightful about her guitar?"

"Oh, when she had that she always sang moony songs, and after that —"

"Well?" demanded Miss Dysart, mischievously.

"Oh, after that," he returned, with an impatient shake of his shoulders, "she was sure to talk sentiment."

His companion laughed merrily. The

faint, almost unconscious feeling of jealousy
which had risen at the mention of this en-
gaging young lady had vanished entirely in
the indifference with which Mr. Tom spoke
of her. She moved her head with a happy
little motion not unlike that with which a
bird plumes itself. Her soft, low laugh did
not really end, but lost itself among the
dimples of her cheeks.

Tom regarded her with shining eyes.

"Not that I should mind some people's
talking sentiment," he said with a smile.

She raised her laughing gaze to his, and,
as their eyes met, the meaning of the look
in his was too plain to be mistaken. She
flushed and paled, dropping her gaze from
his.

"And did nothing especial happen on the
voyage?" she asked, with a strong effort to
regain her careless manner.

"Not that I recall," he answered, putting
his hand beside hers upon the rustic table so
that their fingers almost touched.

A moment of silence followed, broken only
by the chirping of a few belated crickets,
that, despite the advancement of the season,
had not yet discontinued their autumnal con-
certs. The two, so quiet outwardly, sat with
beating hearts, when suddenly a wandering

breeze brought into the summer-house a puff
of smoke from the burning salt meadows. It
was laden with the fetid odor of consuming
animal matter, and so powerful was it that
both involuntarily turned away their heads.

"Bah!" Columbine cried. "How horrible! There must be a dead animal of some
sort there that the fire has reached."

She stopped speaking and gazed with surprise at Tom, who had buried his face in his
hands with a groan.

"What is it? Has it made you ill? It is
gone now."

He lifted a face white with emotion.

"No," he said, "it has not made me ill, —
physically, that is; but it has done worse, it
has made me remember."

"Ah!" she exclaimed. "What is it? is it
so terrible?"

She leaned toward him, and to poor Tom
she looked the incarnation of enticing loveliness. Sympathy and interest — not unmixed,
she being a woman, with curiosity — sparkled
in her eyes, yet he nerved himself to tell her
all that had come back to him.

"That smell of burning hide," he began,
"brought it all up in a flash. The ship got
on fire; Miss Grant clung to me; there was
just such an odor leaking out around the

hatches from the hold where the flames were at the cargo; she — I — when everything else was right, when the fire was out, I was all wrong."

" I do not understand," Columbine said.

She drew away from him, her cheeks pale, her very lips wan. She did not meet his gaze, but sat with downcast eyes.

" I was engaged to Miss Grant. I did not pretend to love her, but I thought we were all bound for the bottom, and " —

He stopped helplessly; her eyes flashed upon him.

" And if a lie would soothe her last moments," she said, bitterly, " you — No, no; I beg your pardon."

" I remember more," he went on, wrenching each word out as if by a strong effort of will. " The shock, and, perhaps, previous seeds of disease, were too much for her father; he died the day before we landed. She was alone in the world, she had no protector, and I — I married her at once, to protect her."

A sparrow flew up into the lattice outside the arbor without noticing the pair within, so dead was the stillness which now fell upon them. At length Columbine rose and stood an instant by the table which had been be-

tween them. She wavered an instant, then
stooped and kissed him upon the forehead.
Then without a word she turned from the
arbor and fled swiftly to the house.

VI.

LEFT alone in the summer-house Tom's
first feeling was a great throb of joy; but
it gave place almost instantly to an aching
pang of misery. To be assured of Columbine's love would have been intense happiness an hour before; now it could only add
to his pain. He raged against the toils in
which fate had entangled him, yet defiance
to helplessness and every paroxysm of rage
at destiny ended in a new and humiliating
consciousness of his own impotence. He felt
like one who walked blindfolded, with light
granted him, not to avoid missteps, but merely
to see them after they were taken.

One thing at least was clear to Tom, — that
he must leave the Dysart mansion. To go
on seeing Columbine day after day, with the
knowledge at once of their love and of the
barrier that stood between them, was a position too painful and too anomalous to be
endured. Both for his own sake and for Miss

Dysart's it was necessary that he delay no
longer. Where he was going he was not at
all clear; that he left to circumstances to
decide. He quitted the arbor and walked
toward the house, so intent upon his painful
thoughts that at a turning of the path he
ran plump against old Sarah, who was hurrying along with a face full of anxiety.

"Oh, mercy gracious, Mr. Thomas!" the
faithful creature cried; "I'm sure I beg your
pardon! But you look as if you'd seen a
ghost!"

"So I have," he answered. "Where are
you going with that spade?"

"To the salt meadows," she answered.
"The fire's sure to come into the lower
garden if we don't ditch it, and if it does,
there'll be no stopping it from the house."

"What!" exclaimed Tom. "Where are
the men?"

"There ain't no men," old Sarah returned,
philosophically. "Why should there be?"

"But you are not going down to ditch
alone?"

"'D I be likely to stop in-doors and let
the house where I've lived fifty years burn
over my head?" demanded she, grimly.

"Give me the spade," was his reply. "A
little work will do me good."

Old Sarah remonstrated, but it ended in
the strangely matched pair going together
to the meadows below.

The dry sphagnum was readily cut through
with the spade, and it was not a difficult,
although a slow task, to dig a wide, shallow
trench between the stretch of burning moss
and the gardens.   Once the ditch was complete, it would be easy to fight the fire on the
home side, since there was nothing swift or
fierce about the conflagration, it being rather
a sullen, relentless smouldering of the moss
and grass-roots, dry from the long drought.

Zealously as the two labored, the fire gained
upon them, and as they worked, they could
not but cast despairing glances at the long
stretch of garden which lay still unprotected.

Meanwhile Columbine from her window
had seen the laborers, and, in a moment realizing the danger, she flew to the library.

"Father," she cried, "the salt marshes
have been burning all day, and the fire is
almost up to the garden."

"Good heavens, Columbine, how impetu-
ous you are!   You have quite driven out of
my head what became of the second son
of—"

"But, father," she interrupted, impatiently,
"do you realize that if you sit here pother-

ing about second sons the house may be burned over our heads?"

"Burned!" exclaimed the genealogist, in dismay; "and all my papers scattered about! Oh, help me, Columbine, to pack up my notes; but don't take up anything without asking me where it goes. Do you think that iron-bound trunk will hold them all?"

Fearing to trust herself to reply, Columbine darted from the library, leaving her father to the half-frenzied collection of his papers, and betook herself to the salt meadows, where, grimed with smoke, Tom and the old serving woman were sturdily laboring. The pungent smoke eddied about them, and already old Sarah's gown showed marks of having been on fire in a dozen places. Columbine stood upon the descending path a moment and regarded them; then, with a step which bespoke determination, she went on and joined them.

"Go back!" shouted Tom, hoarsely, as she approached; "don't you see how the sparks are flying about? You'll be a-fire before you know it."

And, indeed, the fire was becoming more active as it crept nearer to the edges of the meadows, where the grass was taller. The word of warning had hardly left Tom's lips

before she found her dress burning, and
while, being of wool, it was easily extin-
guished, Tom found in it an excuse for taking her in his arms to smother the flame.

"Go back to the house," he said, in a voice
which was full of feeling, yet which it would
have been impossible to disobey. "We shall
save the place; but I cannot work while you
are in danger."

"And you?" she demanded, clasping her
hands upon his arm.

"Nonsense! there is no danger for me,"
he returned, smiling tenderly. "Don't think
of me."

It was not until late in the night that the
contest against the fire was concluded. Tom
worked with an energy in which desperation
had a large place, while old Sarah, with the
pathetic fidelity of an animal, labored by his
side, indefatigable and unmurmuring. Faint
streaks of light had begun to show in the
east when Tom flung down the spade, upon
which he had been leaning, for a last close
scrutiny.

"It is all right now," he said; "there can't
possibly be any fire left on this side of the
marshes. It was lucky for us that the tide
rose into the lower part of the trench."

Undemonstratively, as she had worked, old

Sarah gathered herself together, grimy, stooping, quivering with weariness and hunger, and
crept back to the house they had saved;
while Tom, with tired step, climbed the path
and took his way past the summer-house
toward the other side of the mansion. As he
passed the arbor something stirred within.

"Columbine!" he said, in surprise, recog-
nizing by some instinct that it was she.
"Why, Columbine, what are you here for?
You will be chilled to death."

"You sent me away," returned the girl,
with a trace of dogged protest in her voice.
"You wouldn't let me help."

"I should hope not," laughed Tom, nervously, taking off his hat and passing his hand
through his hair, from which odors of smoke
flowed as he stirred it. "You were hardly
made to fight fire."

"No," she answered, with sudden and sig-
nificant vehemence, "I was not made to fight
fire."

He moved uneasily where he stood in the
darkness; then he took a stride forward and
sat down beside her. They were silent a moment, his eyes fixed upon the first far sign of
dawn, while hers searched the gloom for his
features.

"Columbine," he began, at length, in a

voice of strange softness, " it would have been
better for us both if I had never come here."

" No, no," was her eager reply; " I cannot
have you say that. You have put savor into
my life that was so vapid before."

" But a bitter savor," he said.

" Bitter, yes," Columbine returned in a
voice which, though low and restrained, betrayed the fierceness of her excitement.
" Bitter as death; but sweet too, sweet as — "

She left the sentence unfinished. Below
on the shore the full tide was lapping the
stones with monotonous melody. Save for
their iterance, the stillness was almost as
deep as the marvellous silence of a winter
night which no sound of living thing breaks.

" Whatever comes," Columbine murmured
a moment later, her voice changed and softened so that he had to bend to catch her
words, " I am glad of all that has happened;
glad of you; glad, always glad."

He caught her passionately in his arms
and covered her downcast head with kisses,
while she yielded unresistingly to his embrace, although she sobbed as if her heart
would break. In the east the promise of the
dawn shone steadily, increasing slowly but
surely. It became at last so strong that
Columbine, opening her swollen lids, was

able to distinguish objects a little. At that
moment she became conscious that the arms
of her lover had loosened their hold upon
her. She looked into his face with sudden
alarm. Mr. Tom had fallen into a dead faint.

VII.

THE afternoon sun was shining into Tom's
chamber windows when he awoke. Ten hours
of heavy sleep had had a wonderfully revig-
orating effect upon him, and despite some
stiffness he awoke with a sense of renewed
power. His repose had, too, a far more remarkable effect than this. Before his eyes
were open he said aloud, as if he were solemnly summoning some culprit before the
bar of an awful tribunal : —

" Thomas Wainwright ! "

The sound of his own words acted upon
him like an electric shock. He started up
in bed, wide awake, his eyes shining, his
whole manner alert, joyous, and confident.
He was nameless no longer. Treacherous
memory had yielded up its tenaciously kept
secret, and at last he emerged from the shadowy company of the nameless to be again a
man among men.

He sprang from his couch and made his toilet with impatient eagerness. As he dressed he remembered everything in an instant. That baffling mystery of his family name seemed the key to all the secrets of his past, and, having yielded up this prime fact, his memory made no further resistance. His whole life lay before him, no longer laboriously traced out, bit by bit, but unrolled as a map, visible at a single *coup d'œil.*

Little that he recalled was of a ·nature to change the conclusions he had formed of his circumstances, except the single fact that his wife had not outlived her honeymoon. The shock of her father's death, and, perhaps, some seeds of malaria contracted in India, had proved too much for her delicate constitution, and Tom, eagerly reviewing his newly recovered past, felt a pang of unselfish sorrow for the unloved bride who had for so short a time borne his name, that name which he now kept saying over to himself, as if he feared he might again forget it.

He hurried downstairs, and in the old-fashioned hall, stately with its wainscoting and antique carved furniture, he met Columbine coming towards him. Like his, her eyes shone with a new light, her lips were parted with excitement, and her step was eager.

"Good-morning, Mr. Wainwright," she fluted in a voice high with excitement and joyousness. "I heard your step, and could not wait for you to get to the parlor."

"Good heavens!" cried he, stopping short in amazement. "How did you know? Are you a witch?"

"No," she laughed, pleasure and excitement mingling rather dangerously in her mood. "Nothing of the sort, I assure you; though one of my ancestors was tried for witchcraft at Salem. Cousin Tom sent me this advertisement, and I knew at once that it must be you."

The advertisement she showed him was cut from a New York paper, and called, with a detailed description of the personal appearance of the missing man, for tidings of one Thomas Wainwright, of Baltimore, supposed to have perished in the wreck of the Sound steamer, and whose large estate was unsettled. Tom read it over with mingled feelings.

"Bah!" he said. "When I get home I shall only have to look over a file of the daily papers to read my obituary. Fortunately I have been back from India so few years that they cannot say a great deal about me."

" *De mortuis*," returned Columbine, smiling. " They will only say good of you. I
congratulate you on having found your
name."

" I had it before you told me," he said.

He took her hands in his and looked at
her tenderly.

" I have all my past, too," he went on. " I
am free; I have nothing to hide; nothing
stands between us. Will you be my wife,
Columbine? "

She grew pale as ashes; then flushed celes-
tial red; but her eyes did not flinch.

" I trust you utterly," she answered him.
" And I love you no less."

Interlude First

---◆---

AN EPISODE IN MASK.

AN EPISODE IN MASK.

[*Scene: — A balcony opening by a wide, curtained window from a ball-room in which a masquerade is in progress. Two maskers, the lady dressed as a peasant girl of Britany and her companion as a brigand, come out. The curtains fall behind them so that they are hidden from those within.*]

He. You waltz divinely, mademoiselle.

She. Thank you. So I have been told before, but I find that it depends entirely upon my partner.

He. You flatter me. Will you sit down?

She. Thank you. How glad one is when a ball is over. It is almost worth enduring it all, just to experience the relief of getting through with it.

He. What a world-weary sentiment for one so young and doubtless so fair.

She. Oh, everybody is young in a mask, and by benefit of the same doubt, I suppose, everybody is fair as well.

He. It were easy in the present case to settle all doubts by dropping the mask.

She. No, thank you. The doubt does not trouble me, so why should I take pains to dispel it? Say I am five hundred; I feel it.

He. What indifference ; and in one who waltzes so well, too. Will you not give me another turn?

She. Pardon me. I am tired.

He. And you can resist music with such a sound of the sea in it?

She. It is not melancholy enough for the sea.

He. Is the sea so solemn to you, then?

She. Inexpressibly. It is just that — solemn. It is too sad for anger, and too great and grave for repining ; it is as awful as fate.

He. I confess it never struck me so.

She. It did not me always. It was while I was in Britany — where I got this peasant dress ; isn't it quaint? — that I learned to know the sea. It judged me ; it reiterated one burden over and over until it seemed to me that I should go mad ; yet at the same time its calmness gave me self-control. If there had been the slightest trace of anger or relenting in its accusations, I could have turned away easily enough, and shaken its influence all off. But it was like an awful tribunal before which I had to stand silent, and review my past as interpreted by inexorable justice, — with no palliations, no shams, nothing but honest truth. But why should I say all this rigmarole to you? You must be amused, — if you are not too much bored, that is.

He. On the contrary, I thank you very much.

She. For what?

He. First, for your confidence in me ; and second, for telling me an experience so like my own.

It was not the sea, but circumstances that delivered me over to myself, — a long, slow convalescence, in which I, too, had an interview with the Nemesis of truth, and found a carefully built structure of shams and self-deception go down as mist before the sun. The most frightful being in the world to encounter is one's estranged better self.

She. That is true. No one but myself could have persuaded me that it was I who was to blame. The more I was argued with, the more I believed myself a martyr, and my husband —

He. Your husband?

She. I have betrayed myself. I am not mademoiselle, but madame.

He. But I see no —

She. No ring? True; I returned that to my husband before I went to Britany.

He. And in Britany?

She. In Britany I would have given the world to have it back again.

He. But your husband? Did he accept it so easily?

She. What else can a man do when his wife casts him off?

He. Do? Oh, it is considered proper in such cases, I believe, for him to make a violent pretence of not accepting his freedom.

She. You seem to be sure he considered it freedom!

He. Pardon me. I forgot for the moment that you were his wife.

She. Compliments do not please me.

He. Then you are not a woman.

She. Will you be serious?

He. Why should I be — at a ball?

She. Because I choose.

He. Oh, good and sufficient reason !

She. But tell me soberly, — you are a man, — what could my husband have done?

He. Do you mean to make my ideas standards by which to try him?

She. Perhaps yes; perhaps no.   At least tell me what you think.

He. A man need not accept a dismissal too easily.

She. But what then?

He. He might have followed; he might have argued. It is scarcely possible that you alone were to blame. Was there nothing in which he might have acknowledged himself wrong, — nothing with which he should reproach himself?

She. How can I tell what took place in his heart? I only know my own. He may have re-pented somewhat, or he may not. As for follow-ing — You do not know my husband. He is just, just, just. It was his one fault, I thought then. It took time for me to appreciate the worth of such a virtue.

He. But what has that to do with following you?

She. 'She has chosen,' he would reason. 'Let the event punish her; it is only right that she should suffer for her own act.'

He. But is his justice never tempered by mercy?

She. The highest mercy is to be just. To palliate is merely to postpone sentence.

He. You are the first woman I ever met who would acknowledge that.

She. Few women, I hope, have been taught by an experience so hard as mine. But how dolefully we are talking. Do say something amusing; we are at a ball.

He. I might give you an epigram for the one with which you served me a moment ago, and retort that to be amusing is to be insincere.

She. Then — for we came to be amused — why are we here?

He. Manifestly because we prize insincerity.

She. You are right. I came to get away from myself. One must do something, and even the dissipations of charity pall after a time.

He. We seem to be in much the same frame of mind, and perhaps cannot do better than to stay where we are, consorting darkly, while the others take pains to amuse themselves. So we get through the evening, that is the main thing.

She. You have forgotten to be as complimentary as you were half an hour since.

He. Have I? And yet the greatest compliment a man can pay a woman is sincerity.

She. If he does not love her, yes.

He. Ah, then you agree with Tom Moore :

> " While he lies, his heart is yours ;
> But oh ! you 've wholly lost the youth,
> The instant that he tells you truth ! "

She. Perhaps ; but it is no matter, since we were not talking of love.

He. But if we were?

She. If we were we should undoubtedly say a great many foolish things and quite as many false ones.

He. You are cynical.

She. Oh, no. Cynicism is like a cravat, very becoming to a man if properly worn, but always setting ill upon a lady.

He. Did you learn that, also, in Britany? It is a country of enlightenment. Would that my wife had gone there.

She. Or her husband !

He. You are keen. Her husband learned bitter truths enough by staying at home. I am evidently your complement ; for I had a wedding-ring sent back to me.

She. And why?

He. Why? Why? Who ever knows a woman's reason ! Because I refused, perhaps, to call black white, to say I was pleased by what made me angry ; because — No ; on the whole, since I am not making love to her, it is hardly worth while to lie to a peasant from Britany, though it is of course necessary to sustain the social fictions with people nearer home. It was because the wedding-ring was a fetter that constrained my wife, body and soul; because I was as inflexible as steel. My purposes, my views, my beliefs were the Procrustean bed upon which every act of hers was measured. *Voila tout!*

She. I understand, I think.

He. Oh, I have learned well enough where the blame lay in the three years since she left me.

She. Three years!

He. Why do you start?

She. It is three years, too, since I —

He. Who are you?

She. It is no matter; my husband is far from here.

He. That is more than I can say of my wife.

She. Where is she, then?

He. Heaven knows; not I. But let that go. Why may we not be useful to each other? Our cases are similar; we are both lonely.

She. And strangers.

He. Acquaintance is not a matter of time, but of temperament. Should we have found it possible to be so frank with one another had we been merely strangers?

She. You are specious.

He. No; only honest.

She. But what —

He. What? Why, friendship. We have found

it possible to be frank in masks; why not out of them?

She. Then you propose a platonic friendship?

He. I want a woman who will be my friend, to whom I can talk freely. There are words a man has no power or wish to say to a man, yet which must be spoken or they fester in his mind.

She. I am, then, to be a safety-valve.

He. Every man must have a woman as a lode-star; you are to be that to me.

She. And your wife?

He. My wife? She voluntarily abandoned me. I have n't seen her for three years; and surely she ought to cease to count by this time.

She. You are heartless.

He. Heartless?

She. You should be faithful to your lost —

He. Lost fiddlestick!

She. You are very rude!

He. I don't see —

She. And very disagreeable.

He. But —

She. If you had really loved your wife, you 'd always mourn for her, whatever she did.

He. Good Heavens! That is like a woman. A man is expected to bear anything, everything, and if at last he does not come weeping to kiss the hand that smites him, he is heartless, forsooth! Bah! I am not a whipped puppy, thank you.

She. Your love was, perhaps, never distinguished by meekness?

He. I 'm afraid not.

She. It might be none the worst for that. The ideal man for whom I am looking will not be too lamblike, even in love.

He. You look for an ideal man, then?

She. As closely as did Diogenes.

He. And your husband?

She. Oh, like your wife, he should, perhaps, begin not to count.

He. Good. We are sworn friends, then, until you find your ideal man.

She. If you will.

He. Then unmask.

She. Is that in the bargain?

He. Of course. Else how should we know each other again?

She. But —

He. Unmask !

She. Very well, — when you do.

He. Now, then. [*They unmask.*]

She. Philip !

He. Agnes !

She. You knew all the time !

He. Who told you I was here?

She. I did n't know it.

He. I thought you went to Russia.

She. Well, I did n't. I hope you feel better ! Good night.

5

He. Wait, Agnes. I —

[*There is a moment's silence, in which they look at each other intently.   He takes her hand in both his.*]

He. Agnes, I am not your ideal man, but —

She. Nor I your ideal woman, apparently. Your wife does not count, you say.

He. No more than your husband ; so we are quits there.

She. It 's very horrid of you to remind me of that.

He. I acknowledge that I was always very horrid in everything.

She. Oh, if you acknowledge that, Phil, it is hardly worth while to spend any more time in explanations while this divine waltz is running to waste.

He. But you were tired and out of sorts.

She. You old goose, don't you see that I 'm neither !

He. And you do waltz divinely.

[*They attempt to adjust their masks, but somehow get into each other's arms.   In a few moments more, however, they are seen among the dancers within.*]

Tale the Second.

---◆---

THE TUBEROSE.

THE TUBEROSE.

I.

"**I** SHALL feel honored, Mistress Henshaw, if you will accept this posie as a token which may perchance serve to keep me in remembrance while I am over the sea."

"I am extremely beholden to you," replied the old dame addressed, her wrinkled face illuminated with a smile of pleasure. "But for keeping you in remembrance it needs not this posie or other token. I do not hold my friends so lightly."

"I thank you for counting me one of your friends," John Friendleton said frankly. "I have no kindlier memories of Boston than of the home under your roof."

He had placed upon the many-legged table a flower-pot containing a thrifty tuberose, and with a kindly smile upon his handsome and winning face, he stood regarding the old dame into whose custody he had just given the plant. The dress of the period, — the days of the end of the seventeenth cen-

tury, —plain though it was, accorded well
with the sturdy honesty and kindness of his
face and the compact and strong build of
his figure. The wrinkled crone returned
his smile with one of frosty but genuine
warmth.

"This plant is none the less pleasing to
me," she said, "though I by no means need
it as a reminder. I shall be very careful in
its nourishing."

"It is by no means an ordinary herb,"
Friendleton returned lightly. "There may
be magic in it for aught I can tell. My
uncle, who sent me the bulbs from even so
far away as Spain, hath a shrewd name as
a wise man; and to say sooth he belike doth
know far more than altogether becometh a
good Christian. I give you fair warning that
there may be mischief in the herb; though
to be sure," he added laughing, "the earth
in which it grows is consecrated, for I filled
the pot from Copp's Hill graveyard hard by
here."

A momentary gleam shot with a sinister
light its fiery sparkle across the black eyes of
Mistress Henshaw.

"To one who feareth no harm," she answered, "it seldom haps. I trust the wind
may hold fair for your sailing," she added,

glancing from the small-paned window, "and that you may safely return to Boston as you are minded."

"Thank you, I have hitherto been much favored by Providence in my journeyings. Farewell, Mistress Henshaw."

The old dame received his adieu, and a moment later she watched from the window his active young figure as he walked briskly away. She regarded it intently until a corner hid him from sight. Then she turned back to her room and her occupations.

"Providence, indeed!" she muttered half aloud, with a world of contempt in her tone.

Then she turned to the thrifty, healthy tuberose and caressed its leaves with her thin old fingers as if it were alive and could understand her attentions.

The house in which this conversation took place was still standing a few years since, the oldest in Boston, at the corner of Moon and Sun Court streets. It was erected in 1669; its timber, tradition says, being cut in the neighborhood. The upper story projected over the lower like a frowning brow, from beneath which the windows shone at night like the glowing eye-balls of a wild beast. It was a stout and almost warlike-looking edifice, which preserved even up to the day when, in 1878, it was at length pulled down by the hand of progress, a certain strongly individual appearance, which if less marked at the time when John. Friendleton bade Mistress Henshaw good-by, and the building was thirty years old, must always have distinguished the dwelling from those about it.

Dwellings, however, take much of their air from dwellers, and Mistress Henshaw was likely to impart to any house she inhabited a bearing unlike that of its neighbors. She was a dame to all appearances of some three score winters, each frosty season having left its snow upon her hair. Her figure was still erect, while her eyes were piercing and black and capable of a glance of such strength and directness as almost to seem supernatural.

It may have been from the power and fervor of this glance that Mistress. Henshaw acquired the uncanny reputation which she enjoyed in Boston. As she moved with surprising energy about the house, overseeing and directing her dumb negro servant Dinah, the eyes of passers-by who saw her erect figure flit by the windows were half averted as if from some deadly thing which yet held them with a weird fascination ; and at nightfall the children whom chance belated in the neighborhood went skurrying past Dame Henshaw's house like frightened hares.

It is not perhaps to be told why Satan should have been able to establish his kingdom among a people so devout and pious as the godly inhabitants of the Massachusetts colony; yet we have it upon the testimony of no less a man than the sage and reverend Cotton Mather, whose sepulchre is with us unto this day, and upon the word of many another scarcely less wise and devout, that the Father of Evil did establish a peculiar and covenant people of his own in the midst of the very elect of New England. It may be that it is always as it was in the days of Job, and that the sons of God never assemble without finding in their midst the dark form of Lucifer; for certain it is that the devil, to quote the Rev. Cotton Mather's own words, " broke in upon the country after as astonishing a manner as was ever heard of."

" Flashy people," quaintly and solemnly remarks the learned divine, " may burlesque these things, but when hundreds of the most sober people in a country where they have as much *mother-wit* certainly as the rest of mankind, know them to be *true*, nothing but the absurd and forward spirit of *Sadducism* can question them." From all of which,

and from much more which might be cited, it
is evident that there was plenty of witchcraft
abroad in those days, whether Mistress Henshaw was concerned therein or not.

It is sufficient to note that certain gossips
scrupled not to declare that Dame Henshaw
was one of the accursed who bore the mark
of the beast and kept tryst at the orgies
of the witches' sabbath, and the report once
started the facts in the case made little difference. Some of her neighbors went so far
as to declare that if the dame's residence
were forcibly changed from Sun Court street
to Prison lane, the community would be the
better off.

Governor Belamont, however, in this last
year of the century, was far more exercised
about pirates than concerning witches; and
better pleased at the capture of Captain Kidd,
who had just fallen into his hands, than if he
had discovered all the wise women in the
colonies. Public feeling, moreover, was still
in a reactionary state from the horrors of the
Salem delusion of 1692; and thus it came
about that Mistress Henshaw was left un-
molested.

The second person in the dialogue given
above, John Friendleton, was an Englishman,
and, if tradition be true, the son of an old

lover of Mistress Henshaw. He had taken
up his abode with that lady upon his arrival
in the New World, whither he had been led,
like many another stout young blade of his
day, by the hope of finding fair fortunes in
the growing colonies, and from the first he
had been a favorite with the old lady. It
was whispered over certain of those tea-cups
which we now tenderly cherish from a re-
spect for the memory of very great grand-
mothers and an æsthetic enjoyment of the
beauties of old china, that it was by the aid
of unhallowed power exercised in his behalf
that the young man was always so fortunate
in his undertakings. There were sinister tales
of singular coincidences which had worked
for his good, and behind which the gossips
believed to lie the instigating will of his
powerful landlady. Whether he himself was
aware of this supernatural aid, opinion was
divided, but he was so frank and handsome
withal that the weight of opinion leaned
toward acquitting him. The habit of New
England thought, moreover, was so opposed
to imagining a witch as exercising her power
for anything but evil, that these rumors after
all gained no great or general credence.

The friendship between the dame and her
lodger was perhaps based upon mutual need.

The young man gave her that full confidence
which a pure-minded youth enjoys bestowing
upon an elderly female friend; while in turn
the childless old lady, alone and otherwise
friendless, regarded him with tender affection.   She cherished any chance token from
him, and especially did she seem touched by
this gift of a tuberose which he had given her
at parting.   She knew how carefully he had
tended and cherished the plant, more rare
then than now, and long after the sails of the
ship which conveyed him to England, whither
he had been summoned by the serious illness
of a relative, had dipped under the horizon,
the old witch — if witch she were — sat regarding the flower with eyes in which the
tears glistened.

.

II.

It was early springtime when John Friendleton once more caught sight of the beacon
upon Trimountain, and the walls of the fort
standing upon a hill which has itself been removed by the enterprise of Boston.   The few
months of the young man's absence, and the
progress of time from one century to another
— for it was now 1700 — had brought no

great changes to the town; but to him it
seemed far from being the same he had left.

The first tidings he had received from Boston, after landing in England, had been a
letter telling of the death of Mistress Henshaw. She had set out from Boston, so
the letter informed him, to visit a sister living
somewhere in the wilds toward far Pemaquid,
and had never returned. The letter was
written by one Rose Dalton, who claimed
to be a niece of the deceased, and who
had come into possession of the small prop-
erty of Mistress Henshaw by virtue of a
will made before the adventurous and fatal
journey. The writer added to her letter the
information that she should live on with
dumb Dinah, holding as nearly as possible
to the fashion of her aunt's housekeeping.

When John stood once more upon the well-
remembered threshold, he felt half disposed
to turn away and enter no more a place in
which every familiar sight could but call up
sad memories. Then, endeavoring to shake
off his melancholy, he knocked.

A light, brisk step approached from within,
and the door opened quickly.

John stood in amazement, unable to utter
a word, so bewildered was he by the beauty
of the maiden who stood before him; a

beauty which now, after nearly two centuries, is still a tradition of marvel. Something unreal and almost supernatural there might seem in the wonderful loveliness of this exquisite creature, were it not that she seemed so to overflow with life and vitality. Her soft and dove like eyes were full of gleams of human energy, of joy, of passion; she had all the beauty of a perfect dream without its unreality; and then and there the young Englishman's heart fell down and worshipped her, never after to swerve from its allegiance.

"You must be Mr. Friendleton," the maiden said, courtesying bewitchingly. "I knew your ship was in."

"I — I have been minding my luggage," he stammered, rather irrelevantly, his eyes fastened upon her face.

"Be pleased to enter," said she, smiling a little at the boldness and unconsciousness of his stare. "Your room has been preserved as you left it at your departure. My aunt, good Mistress Henshaw, as I wrote you, straitly enjoined in her will that everything should be kept for you as you had left it. Her affections were marvellously set upon you."

That he should be allowed to enter under

the same roof with this beautiful creature seemed to John Friendleton the height of bliss, and he had no words to express his delight when he learned that Mistress Rose expected him to take up his abode there as in former times. Her aunt had wished it; had especially spoken of it in her will, and so it was to be.

It would be impossible to pretend that Friendleton struggled much against this proposition, when inclination so strongly pleaded for the carrying out of the wishes of his dead friend; and in this way he became the lodger of young Mistress Rose.

III.

It did not long escape the eye of the young man that his new landlady wore always at her throat a cluster of the white, waxy blossoms of the tuberose. The circumstance was in itself sufficiently curious and unusual to excite his attention, and it recalled to his mind the plant he had given to Mistress Henshaw. He wondered what had been the fate of his gift, and one day he ventured to ask Mistress Rose about it. For reply she led him to the room formerly occu-

pied by her aunt, and showed him the tuberose in a quaint pot. It had grown tall and
thrifty, and half a dozen slim stalks upon it
stood up stoutly, covered with buds, which
showed here and there touches of dull red
evolved in their transformation from green to
white.

"I marvel how it hath increased," John
said.

"It hath thriven marvellously," she replied.
"Never before hath it been known that the
plant would bloom throughout all the year,
but this sends out buds continually. I daily
wear a blossom, as you may see, and I find
its odor wonderfully cheering, although for
most it is too powerfully sweet."

"It is an ornament which becometh you
exceedingly well," he responded, flushing.

"My neighbors," returned she smiling,
"regard it as exceeding frivolous."

The fragrance of the flower which Mistress
Rose wore at her throat floated about John
wherever his daily occupations led him, and
doubly did the delicious perfume steal through
his dreams. He never thought of the maiden
without feeling in the air that divinely sweet
odor; and a thousand times he secretly compared her to the flower she wore. Nor was
the comparison inapt; since her beauty was

rendered somewhat unearthly by the strange
pallor of her face, while the intense and
passionate intoxication it produced might,
without great straining of the simile, be directly compared to the exaltation which the
delicious and powerful fragrance produces
in sensuous and sensitive natures.

The intimacy between the young people
was at first hindered by the shyness of
Friendleton, who was only too conscious of
the fervor and depth of his passion; but as
Rose had many of the well-remembered ways
of her aunt, and, stranger yet, appeared well
versed in his own past history, he soon
became more at his ease. In defiance of
the proverb which condemns all true lovers
to uneven ways and obstructed paths, the
wooing of lovely Mistress Rose by John
Friendleton ran smoothly and happily on,
seeming to have begun with the young man's
first meeting with his lovely landlady. The
gossips of Boston town, strangely enough,
left the relations of the lovers untouched
by any but friendly comment; and in a fashion as natural as the ripening of the year,
their love ripened into completeness.

It was early autumn when Rose became
Mistress Friendleton. The wedding was quietly celebrated in the old North Church,

and never in its century of existence before
its timbers went to feed the campfires of
British soldiers, did that house shelter a
more lovely bride or a more manly and
blissful groom. A faint flush softened the
pallor of the maiden, the one charm which
could add to her beauty. Her only ornament was her usual cluster of tuberoses, and
more than one spectator noted how like the
flower was the lady. The circumstance was
recalled afterward when the slab was placed
above her grave in Copp's Hill burial-ground.
There still lingers among certain old gossips
of tenacious memory the tradition of a stone
which had on it "some sort of a flower." It
was the slab upon which John Friendleton,
imaginative at sorest need, had caused to be
carved simply a bunch of tuberoses.

If John had been happy in anticipation, he
was, if such a thing be possible, no less so in
reality. It is as trite to attempt as it is impossible to effect the portraying of the life
of two young people who are profoundly
happy in each other. Joy may be named,
but not painted. Even were it easy to picture their existence, their self-absorption
would prevent their being interesting. As
I have sometimes passed the old house on
Moon Street, standing worn and stained with

the storms of two centuries, a picture has risen before me of the young bride and groom sitting together and inhaling the fragrance of a quaint pot of tuberoses, blooming so wonderfully that the whole house was filled with their odor; and the memory brings always the tears to my eyes.

IV.

NOVEMBER was at its last day. A severe storm, half rain, half snow, was sweeping over Boston. The beacon upon Trimount trembled in the blast, and on the shores of the peninsula the waves roared sullenly. Few people were abroad, and there was never a watchman in the city who did not for that day at least regret having chosen a calling which kept him out of doors in such weather.

The house on Sun Court Street was too stoutly built to tremble, yet those within heard the wind howling over the hill as if scourged by all the furies. It was one of those nights when a man sits before his fire and realizes the value of all his blessings.

John and Rose sat together before the blazing hearth while the husband told stories of his boyhood in England. The wife

nestled close to him, absorbed in the narration, yet not forgetting to fondle his hand
with her smooth, soft fingers.

Suddenly into the room burst black, dumb
Dinah, wringing her hands and moving her
speechless lips with frightful earnestness.
In her hands she carried the fragments of
the pot which had held the tuberose.

Rose sprang up with a cry of anguish.

" Dinah! Dinah! My tuberose ! "

The negress gesticulated wildly, but her
mistress rushed past her; and, followed by
her husband, hastened to see for herself the
extent of the mischief.

The pot had been overturned by the wind,
which had burst in one of the tiny greenish
window panes, and the plant was completely
crushed in the downfall. Not a single flower
had escaped, and mingled with fragments of
pottery and with the black church-yard mould
in which the flower had — perhaps ill-fatedly
— been planted, were the leaves and petals,
torn and stained and mangled.

In the first sorrow of the discovery of the
accident, Rose threw herself into her husband's arms and burst into tears; but she
soon controlled herself, and became perfectly
calm. She directed Dinah to remove the
débris, and returned to listen to her husband's

stories; and, although she was more quiet than before, she seemed no less interested.

It was late when they prepared to retire.

"John," Rose said, hesitatingly, as they lingered a moment side by side before the wide hearth, ".it is just a year to-night since Mistress Henshaw died. If you are willing; I wish to pass the night alone in her room."

"I am always willing you should do whatever pleaseth you best," he answered, smiling upon her; "but why do you mean to shut me out from your sorrow? I, too, loved her."

"I know," Rose returned, bending to kiss the hand he had laid upon hers, "and I fear you can never be shut out from my sorrows, however much I could wish to spare you. Still, I wish it to be so for to-night."

"Then let it be so. The storm does not fright you?"

"The storm does not fright me."

She took from her throat the tuberoses she had worn that day, and gazed at them sadly.

"I can never wear another," she said. "These are faded like our happy days."

"You speak but sadly," returned her husband, with a look of such fondness that the tears started into her eyes despite all her efforts to restrain them. "You would have

spoken so had you been bidding me farewell.
The destruction of the flower makes you
downcast. Mayhap there is still life in the
root, and it may be made once more to grow
and bloom."

"John," his wife said abruptly, "John, I
have loved you from the first moment I saw
you; I love you now, and I shall love you to
all eternity. Whatever happens, remember
that and believe it."

"I have never doubted that you love me,"
.he answered, gathering her into his arms;
"how else could it be that you could have
made me so utterly happy?"

She clung to him passionately a moment.
Then with an evident effort at self-control,
she kissed his lips fervently, disengaged herself from his embrace, and turned away.

"Good-night, dear," she said.

Then upon the threshold of Mistress Henshaw's chamber she paused and looked back,
tears shining in her beautiful dark eyes.

"Good-night," she repeated; "good-night."

V.

IT was somewhat past his usual hour of
rising when John Friendleton next morning
came downstairs. The storm was over, but

everywhere had it left its traces in broken boughs, overturned fences, and dilapidated chimneys, so that as he looked from the window, John could see on all sides the evidences of its violence.

The house was strangely quiet, and he looked about him with the impatience of a lover for his wife, that she might chase away the unaccustomed sombreness which seemed to have descended upon the place.

" Dinah," he asked, " has not your mistress risen? "

The mute regarded him with a strange appearance of wildness and terror, but she replied by a shake of the head, — instantly hurrying out of the room as if in fear.

John looked after her an instant in bewilderment, not understanding her odd manner; and then approaching the door of the room occupied by his wife, he tapped softly.

There was no response.

He tapped again somewhat more loudly. Still there was no reply. A third time he rapped, now with a heavy hand. All within was as silent as the grave.

Startled by he knew not what fear, with a sudden impulse he set his strong shoulder to the door, and strained until with a crash it flew open.

The heavy curtains were undrawn, and a grey gloom filled the chamber. A fearful silence followed the crash of the breaking lock, and met him like a palpable terror. He saw Rose lying on the bed, her face buried in the pillows; and by some fantastic jugglery, the light from the open door, as it fell upon her hair, — those abundant tresses whose rich, dark glory he so loved, — seemed to silver them to the whiteness of hoary age.

"Rose!" he cried, starting forward to seize her hand which lay upon the coverlid.

The hand was cold with a chill which smote him to the very heart.

"Rose! Sweetheart!" he cried in a piercing voice, bending over and tenderly turning her dear face up to the light.

What horrible mockery confronted him? He started back like one stung by a serpent!

Along the pillow lay a crushed and withered tuberose, and he looked upon the face, ghastly in death, and old and haggard and wrinkled — of Mistress Henshaw.

Interlude Second.

AN EVENING AT WHIST.

AN EVENING AT WHIST.

[The scene is the parlor of a modern house, much adorned, and furnished with a wealth of bric-a-brac, which renders getting about a most difficult and delicate operation, unless one is wholly regardless of the consequences to the innumerable ornaments. Mrs. Greeleigh Vaughn, a corpulent and well-preserved widow, who passes for forty, and is not less, has just seated herself at the whist-table, with her daughter and two guests. One of these, Mr. Amptill Talbot, is one of those young men whose wits seem to be in some mysterious fashion closely connected with the parting of their hair exactly in the middle; the other is a handsome and keen-eyed gentleman of middle age, who answers to the name Colonel Graham.]

Mrs. Vaughn. I am so glad you could and would come, Colonel Graham. Now we shall have a delightful evening at whist. You are such a superb player that I am sure I shall learn more about the game by playing with you a single evening than I should by studying the books for a year.

Colonel Graham. You are too good. I make not the slightest pretence of —

Mrs. V. Oh, of course not. You are too modest; but everybody says that you are a wonderful player. I only hope you won't be too hard on me if I make a mistake.

Miss Vaughn. Oh, I am so glad mamma is your partner, Colonel Graham. I should be frightened to death if I had to play with you. Mr. Talbot will be a good deal more merciful, I am sure.

Mr. Talbot. Anything you do is sure to be right, Miss Vaughn. If you can put up with me, I am sure I can afford to overlook any mistakes you make. I play whist so seldom that I am all out of practice.

Miss V. (dealing). Oh, I just never play, only when I have to make up the table. I have so many things on hand. Why were n't you at the Wentworths' last night, Mr. Talbot?

Mr. T. I was out of town. I think you gave yourself two cards that time.

Miss V. Oh, dear ! Have I made a misdeal? I wish you 'd count your cards.

Colonel G. You are right. The next card is mine.

Miss V. Thank you.

Mrs. V. That came out all right.

Colonel G. But the trump is not turned.

Miss V. Oh, which was the last card? I am sure I don't know; I 've got them all mixed up now.

Mrs. V. Well, never mind. Let me draw one. That will do just as well.

Mr. T. Diamonds? Can't you draw again? I have n't —

Miss V. I don't think it was diamonds. I am almost sure it was spades.

Mrs. V. No, diamonds suits me, and of course you can't change it now ; can she, Colonel Graham ?

Colonel G. It is n't customary, I believe, unless we are to play Auction Pitch, and bid for the trump.

Miss V. Oh, now you are going to be sarcastic ! I don't think that 's fair.

Mrs. V. Do you put your trumps at one end of your hand, Colonel Graham ?

Colonel G. No, I do not, but some people find it a convenience.

Mr. T. Is it my lead ?

Colonel G. No, it is my partner's.

Mrs. V. Oh, is it my lead ? I 'm sure I don't know what to play. You always lead from your long suit, don't you ? There, I. hope that queen will be good.

Mr. T. No, it won't, for I have the ace.

Mrs. V. Oh, you mean man ! Partner, can't you trump that ?

Colonel G. I have suit.

Miss V. There, I have got to put the king on, and I think it is mean.

Mr. T. I am awfully sorry. If I 'd only known —

Miss V. I shook my head at you, but you would n't look up.

Mrs. V. That was n't fair, and you deserve to be beaten. Now my jack is good, any way.

Mr. T. It is n't your lead. I took the trick.

Mrs. V. Oh, I beg pardon.

Miss V. I would have trumped it, any way.

Mr. T. I wish I knew what you have.

Miss V. I wish I could tell you. Don't make it too dark.

Mr. T. Then I'll lead diamonds.

Miss V. That's just right.

Mrs. V. Diamonds are trumps.

Miss V. Oh, are they? Oh, that's too bad. I did n't want trumps led.

Mr. T. But you said — Why, can't you go over Colonel Graham's nine-spot?

Miss V. I made a mistake. I meant to play the ten.

Mrs. V. Shall I put on a small one or a high one, Colonel Graham?

Colonel G. The trick is ours as it lies.

Mrs. V. Then if I put on a high one it will get it out of the way, so you 'll know what to do next time.

Mr. T. Why, you 've thrown away the king of trumps !

Mrs. V. Was n't that right?

Miss V. Why, of course not, mamma. You ought to have put on either the ace or a low one.

Colonel G. It is your lead, Mrs. Vaughn.

Mrs. V. She says she 'll trump hearts, and I can't play my knave. I 'll try spades. I hope you 'll take it.

Mr. T. And he did. How nice to have a partner do just what you tell him to.

Miss V. That means that I don't.

Mr. T. You are always satisfactory, whatever you do.

Miss V. What was led? Clubs? Are clubs trumps?

Colonel G. No ; diamonds.

Miss V. Second hand low. I know that, at any rate, so there's a two-spot.

Mr. T. Your mother has taken it with the seven.

Miss V. Oh, and I had the ace, king, and queen. Ought I to have played one of those?

Colonel G. If you tell us your hand you must expect us to play to it.

Miss V. I did n't mean to tell.

Mrs. V. (*leading spades*). That was your suit, was n't it?

Mr. T. But I hold the ace.

Miss V. It was your own lead, mamma. Any way, I'll trump it.

Mr. T. Why, you've trumped my ace.

Miss V. Oh, did I? I did n't mean to. Can't I take it back?

Colonel G. It is a little late, but still —

Miss V. Oh, well, never mind. Let it go. I have the king, any way (*leading it*).

Colonel G. But you just trumped a spade.

Mrs. V. A revoke ! That gives us three points.

Miss V. Oh, it does n't either ! I did n't see that king at all when I trumped, and that was the only spade I had. I 'll change it on the last trick, and then it will be all right.

Mrs. V. You can't do that; can she, Colonel Graham?

Colonel G. It is n't customary.

Mr. T. Oh, who wants to play the stiff club rules? I don't; there is n't any fun in whist if you are going to be so particular.

Miss V. Whose lead is it now?

Colonel G. If it is n't yours it must be Mr. Talbot's, as you decide about that trick.

Mr. T. Then I 'll lead a spade, and you can trump it.

Miss V. There, that 's better than having that trump wasted on your ace.

Mrs. V. Did you ever play Stop? We played it last summer at Bar Harbor. It 's a Western game, and you have chips, just like poker; and then you stop it if you have the stop cards; and sometimes you 'll have the meanest little cards left in your hands, and if it is the ace of diamonds you have to pay five chips for it, or the king, or the queen, or the knave, or the ten; not so much, of course, but it all counts up awfully fast.

Mr. T. Why, that is ever so much like Sixty-six. Do you remember the time we tried to play Sixty-six on the Bar Harbor boat, Miss Vaughn?

Miss V. Oh, yes; and Ethel Mott *was* such fun. She just would cheat, and there was no stopping her.

Colonel G. It is your lead, Miss Vaughn.

Mrs. V. Oh, just wait a moment. I want to know if fourth best has anything to do with playing fourth hand?

Colonel G. Nothing whatever.

Mr. T. Oh, fourth best is one of those things they 've put in to make whist scientific. For my part, I don't think there 's any fun —

Miss V. That 's just what I say. When I play whist I want to have a good time, and not feel as if I were going through an examination at a scientific school. Oh, did you know we are going to have a whist figure at Janet Graham's german, Mr. Talbot? Won't that be fun?

Mr. T. I am sure then that you 'll be trump.

Miss V. Thank you.

Mrs. V. How pretty !

Colonel G. It is your lead, Miss Vaughn.

Miss V. Why, did I take the last trick? What shall I — oh, I know, — the ace of clubs.

Mrs. V. The two-spot of diamonds ought to be good for that.

Miss V. How horrid ! Now the rest of my clubs are n't any good. Well, any way, I can throw them away.

Mrs. V. Have hearts been led?

Mr. T. I 'm sure I can't remember.

Miss V. (*examining tricks*). Yes, here 's one heart trick.

Mrs. V. Well, I must lead it, and I 'm sure I

don't remember about it at all. I 'll lead a small one. Was that right, Colonel Graham?

Colonel G. You might have led your knave.

Mrs. V. Why, how did you know I had the knave. I declare, it 's like witchcraft, the way you keep run of the cards. I suppose you know where every card is. Who took that?

Colonel G. I did.

Mr. T. I ought to have trumped that, but I do hate to trump second hand.

Colonel G. But you played suit.

Mr. T. So I did. I forgot that.

Colonel G. (*showing hand*). The rest of the tricks are mine.

Miss V. Why, I have the king and queen of clubs, and you have n't a club in your hand.

Colonel G. That is why the tricks are mine. I can keep the lead to the end. I am very sorry, Mrs. Vaughn; but I am suddenly attacked with a nervous headache, so that I cannot possibly go on playing. I shall have to ask to be excused.

Mrs. V. Oh, don't break up the game when we are getting along so well.

Colonel G. I am very sorry; but I must go. I have enjoyed the game extremely.

Mr. T. Are you out?

Colonel G. Yes.

Mrs. V. I 'm sure it was all owing to you.

Colonel G. It was all owing to the fall of the cards. I have n't done anything.

Miss V. I 'm sure we did n't have anything on our side at all. I hate whist anyway; you have to be so quiet, and study on it so.

Mr. T. Yes, I think it 's awfully hard work.

Colonel G. Oh, you 'll have better luck next time. Good-by; don't rise.

[*And the Colonel goes to the club to relieve his mind by a quantity of vigorous expletives, and then to settle down to an evening of what he calls real whist.*]

Tale the Third.

SAUCY BETTY MORK.

SAUCY BETTY MORK.

I.

"**B**UT, Miss Bessie — "

"I have told you a dozen times, Mr. Granton, that my name is not Bessie. I abhor that final *ie* ; and more than that, I was christened Betty, — plain Betty, — and Betty I will be."

"Miss Betty, then, if that suits you; though why you should be so particular about that old-fashioned name, I'm sure I can't conceive."

"In the first place, it is my name," Betty replied, bending upon him a glance at once bewitching and tantalizing; "that ought to count for something; and in the second place, my family name isn't one that lends itself to soft prefixes. Besides all which, there has been a Betty Mork from time immemorial; and I shall never be one to spoil the line by changing my name."

"What?" Mr. Granton demanded mischievously. "Never change it? Are you vowed to eternal single blessedness, then, or shall you imitate the women's-rights women, who — "

" It is really none of your affair what I intend to do," returned she, bridling; " only, to go back to what we started on, I do intend to play in the tournament with Frank Bradford. I am not in the habit of breaking my promises."

The pair walked along the shady country road without speaking for a moment or two, the young man inclined to be sulky, his companion saucy and good-natured. The dropping sunshine, falling through the gently waving elm-boughs, struck golden lights out of Miss Mork's abundant chestnut hair, — her one beauty, it amused her to call it, although the smile which brought out her dimples and the lustre of her eyes contradicted the words even while they were being spoken. Young Granton was fully alive to the attractiveness of the lithe figure beside him; indeed, for his own peace of mind, far too keenly. He was aware, too, of the difficulty of managing the wilful beauty, whose independence was sufficiently understood by all the summer idlers at Maugus.

" But you certainly knew I expected you to play in the tournament with me," he began again, returning to the attack.

" It is n't modest for a girl ever to know

what a man expects of her until she's told,"
Betty replied demurely, "even in tennis.
And besides, it was presumptuous for you to
be so royally certain of my acquiescence in
whatever you deigned to plan."

"I'll serve a cut so that you'll never be
able to return it," threatened he.

"I can serve a cut myself," she retorted,
with an accent which seemed to indicate a
double significance in the words.

"Confound it!" he said, incisively, with
sudden and inconsistent change of base, "it
is perfect folly letting ladies into a tournament anyway. Who wants them? They
always make trouble."

"I understood that you wanted one," Betty
answered, unmoved, observing the fringe of
her parasol with great apparent interest;
"but of course I knew your invitation was not
to be taken too seriously."

"Oh, bother!" the young man cried, slash-
ing viciously at the head of a late-blooming
daisy. "Why do you always insist on quarrelling with me?"

"Are we really quarrelling?" she laughed
back with her most exasperating lightness of
manner. "How delightful! If there is one
thing that I enjoy more than I do tennis, it is
a good quarrel."

"Tennis!" Granton retorted, the last shreds of his patience giving way. "It must be allowed that you can quarrel better than you can play. No girl," he went on, with increasing acerbity, ".can ever really play tennis: she only plays at playing it; and it spoils any man's game to play with her. For my part, I cannot see why they are to be admitted to the tournament at all."

"*Merci!*" exclaimed Mistress Betty, stopping in the sun-dappled way to make him a profound courtesy. "Now I know what your true sentiments -are, and how much your invitation was worth. Thank you for nothing, Mr. Nat Granton. I wish you luck of your partner, — when you get one. It is a cruel shame that by the rules of the tournament it must be a girl!"

And before Granton was able to reply or knew what she intended, pretty Miss Mork, with her tripping gait, her bright eyes, ugly name, and all, had whisked through a turnstile and was half-way across the lawn of the cottage where her particular bosom-friend Miss Dora Mosely was spending the summer.

II.

WHILE Granton continued his perturbed way down the lovely village street to the Elm House, which for the time being was the home of a pleasant colony of summer idlers seeking rest and diversion in Maugus, Miss Betty flitted lightly over the lawn and joined her friend, whom she found reposing in a hammock swung under the cool veranda.

"Oh, Dolly," was her breathless salutation, "I've got the awfullest thing to do! But I'll do it, or perish in the attempt!"

"Halloo, Betty!" was Miss Mosely's response and greeting; "how like a whirlwind you are! What is the matter? What have you got to do?"

"Beat Mr. Granton at tennis in the tournament."

"You and Mr. Bradford, you mean?"

"No; I mean all by myself, — in a single. I sha'n't play in the double at all, if I can get out of it without sneaking."

"What in the world has happened to bring you to this desperate frame of mind?"

"Well, Dolly, the fact is, Mr. Granton has been making himself particularly odious be-

cause I would n't throw over Frank Bradford
to play with him, and — "

"I told you," her friend interrupted judi-
cially, examining the toe of her slipper with
much interest and satisfaction, "that you 'd
be sorry you agreed to play with Frank."

"But I 'm not sorry," protested the other,
with spirit. "Do you think I 'm so bound
up in Nat Granton that I can't get on without him? If he wanted me to play with him
why did n't he ask me, instead of taking it
for granted, in that insufferably conceited
way of his, that I 'd stand about and wait on
his lordship's leisure? Oh, I 'll pay him off!
I shall go over to grandmother's every
blessed day from now until the tournament
and practise, so as to take down his top-lofti-
cal airs."

At which exhibition of spite and determination Miss Mosely fell to laughing, and said
Betty's manner suggested pickled limes,
which in turn reminded her of the chocolate-
creams they had at boarding-school, and that
brought to mind some particularly delicious
marshmallows which had been saved until
Betty should come over; and she added that
it would be a very good plan to go into the
house and devour them.

Over the flabby and inane confection with

which the two friends regaled themselves, it
was arranged that Dora should devote herself
with Machiavelian shrewdness to bringing
about a reconciliation between Frank Bradford and his betrothed, Flora Sturtevant,
whose quarrel had led to the invitation which
had involved Betty in her present difficulties.
In the meantime, Mistress Mork was to give
herself with great assiduity to the practice
of cutting, volleying, and such devices of skill
or cunning as would make possible the realization of her bold plan of conquering Mr.
Granton in the tennis tournament, over which
all the young people were just then much
excited.

These conclusions were not reached without much digression, circumlocution, and irrelevant discourse upon various matters, with
a good deal of consideration of the dress
which would be both convenient and becoming for the important games.

"I have almost a mind to try a divided
skirt," Betty said thoughtfully. "George
saw one at a tournament in England, and it
could be fixed so as not — Oh, Dora, if
George were only here! He knows all the
new English rules and cuts, and all sorts of
quirks. Oh, why did you have to quarrel
with him just now? Now I shall lose my

tennis just because you drove him away from Maugus."

" Why, Betty Mork! You said yourself you would n't stand his lordly ways; you know you did."

" Of course," returned her friend illogically; " but we both agreed that you 'd have to make up with him some time; and I did n't know then that I should want him."

" But what could I do? " demanded Dora, divided between a sense of being deserted by her friend and a desire to have difficulties smoothed over. " Any girl with decent pride would have *had* to send George away. You know how I hated to do it."

" But you might send for him now."

" Oh, I could n't. That would be too awfully humiliating. I wonder you can propose it."

" Men are so dreadful," sighed Betty.

The two forlorn victims of masculine perversity pensively ate marshmallows in silence for a moment, revolving, no doubt, the most profound reflections upon the vanity of human affairs.

" I 'll tell you what I will do," Betty said at length, reflectively. " I 'll write to George and make him visit grandmother. He has n't been there for a year, to stay; and, as grand-

.mother says, she 'admires to have him.' I'll
tell him if he'll stay there, out of sight, I
think I can fix things with you."

"Oh, you delicious, darling hypocrite!"
exclaimed her friend, embracing her raptur-
ously. "You are a perfect treasure, Bet! I'll
do anything to help you, — anything. I've
been perfectly wretched ever since George
went away; but of course I couldn't say so,
if I'd died."

III.

"So you are not going to play with Bradford, after all?" Nat Granton said, flinging
himself on the turf at Miss Mork's feet as she
sat watching the tennis-players practising for
the tournament.

"No," she answered. "He and Flora have
recovered from their temporary alienation,
and I was generous and took myself out of
the way."

"Will you play with me?"

"Thank you; no. I shall not go into any
team; and in any case, I know too well your
sentiments on the subject of girls' playing to
trespass on your good nature."

"Then I shall not play," he said, rather
crossly.

"And pray what do I care if you don't?"

"It would be polite to pretend to, at any rate."

> " 'The slightest approach to a false pretence
> Was never among my crimes ; ' "

she quoted, twirling her gay parasol swiftly on its handle. " Do see Tom Carruth serve. That cut is my despair."

" It is simple enough to return," Granton answered, "if you know when it is coming: you 've only to run up."

" Yes, but how is one to know when it is coming? "

" One always can tell when I give it," he replied, laughing, " for I always fling my head back."

There came a wicked sparkle of intelligence into Betty's eyes as she made a mental note of this confession for future use. Then the long lashes fell demurely over her cheeks as she gathered together her belongings and rose.

" I must go over to grandmother's," she said. " Never spend the summer near your grandmother's, Mr. Granton: she may be ill and absorb all your spare time."

And away sped the deceitful damsel, on nefarious schemes intent, to play tennis with her cousin George, who had responded with celerity to her summons. She was really improving with a good deal of rapidity. She had been a sad romp in her day, and every prank of her tomboy girlhood stood her in good stead now. Every fence and tree she had climbed, to the unspeakable horror and scandal of elderly spinster aunts, every game of ball for which she had been lectured by an eminently proper governess, every stolen fishing-expedition and hoydenish race whose improprieties my lady buried with overwhelming scorn in the oblivion of the past, had been a preparation for the struggle into which she now threw herself with the whole force of mind and body.

Her cousin George Snow, who was sufficiently fond of his mischievous cousin, and duly grateful for her supposed good offices in arranging the difficulties between himself and Dora, was an invaluable ally. He was taken into full confidence, and embraced the project most heartily. Granton was a right nice fellow, he admitted, but it certainly would not hurt him to be taken down a peg. Snow had just returned from England, where he had seen some of the finest tennis-players perform.

"You play too near the net," he said. "All American players do. Play well back, and above everything, put all your force into the return."

"But I shall send the ball out of the court," Betty protested.

"You must n't. Drive it down as hard as ever you can. Strength — or rather swiftness — tells; if your service is swift enough it is worth all the fancy cuts in the world. The Renshaws make half their points by volleying from the service-line, and the rest by swift service."

"Swiftness is the word," Betty returned gayly. "Anything more?"

"Get used to striking back-handed; don't try to turn your thumb down; make a business of an out-and-out back-handed, wrongside-of-the-racquet stroke."

How sound all this advice was, tennis players may determine for themselves; but it certainly served its purpose well. Betty was a promising pupil. Morning, noon, and night she played, working with an assiduity which nearly fagged her cousin out.

"You are plucky, Betty," he declared one day. "I'm afraid for my own laurels. And by the way, am I to be allowed to be present at this great tournament in which you are to cover yourself and your sex with glory?"

"Oh, yes; you are to challenge Mr. Granton if he beats me, — though he sha'n't! Anybody can challenge the winner, you know. That's a provision I had put in myself to cover my own case."

"Poor Granton!" George laughed. "Little does he dream of the awful humiliation in store for him."

Betty set her lips together and nodded her head in a determined way.

"George," she declared, with tragic earnestness, "if I get beaten I shall go straight home and die of — "

"Baffled stubbornness," interpolated her cousin.

"Thwarted vengeance," suggested Dora.

"No, of righteous indignation. Come, one set more before we drive back to Maugus. Only two days left, you know."

IV.

THE morning of the second day of the tournament dawned clear, and what was quite as much to the purpose, unusually cool. A little breeze from the northwest crept over the hills, — just enough to fan the heated players without disturbing the flight of the balls; while to make the weather perfect for tennis, by ten o'clock a light veil of clouds had comfortably covered the sun, cutting off all troublesome rays.

"It is a perfect day," Betty remarked to Dora, as they took their places among the spectators. "I've put my things ready so I can dress in two minutes. Here comes George."

The affair was an event in quiet Maugus. It had been talked about as the most important event could not have been discussed anywhere but in the idle hours of summer leisure, and had come to be regarded as quite the event of the season. The tennis-court was laid out near the Elm House, and was surrounded by superb old trees that in all the slow years of their growth had never over-arched a prettier sight than that afternoon showed, with its groups of nice old ladies, and charming young damsels in all the picturesque bravery of their nineteenth-century costume. The contest of the first day of the tournament had disposed of all the four-handed games but the final match, and the afternoon of the second day was left free for the single games. Granton had entered for the latter, and was looked upon as the probable victor. He won easily his first rubber, and came over to where Betty sat to wait his turn again.

"It is lucky for me, Mr. Snow," he said to George, who in the happiness of full reconciliation sat by Dora's side, "that you are not playing, or I should n't have the ghost of a chance."

"I'm resting on the laurels I won last year," was the light response. "It's far easier than to risk one's reputation and defend it."

"Are you so sure of winning, as it is, Mr. Granton?" asked Betty coolly.

"Sure? Of course not; but I have hopes now, which I should n't indulge if Mr. Snow, with the glory of his victories at Newport last year, were counted in."

"I wish you success," she said, with a certain trace of satire in her tone. "Is n't Mr. Howard playing remarkably well to-day? What a splendid volley? That gives him the game."

"Sets: two, love," called the scorer, and Mr. Howard's victory was saluted with applause, which Mistress Betty took great satisfaction in leading.

"You seem to be greatly pleased at Howard's good luck," Granton observed, remembering that when his success had been clapped, just before, Miss Mork had refrained from lending a hand.

"Why should n't I be?" she returned. "I've bet him a pair of gloves he wins."

"What will you bet me I lose?" demanded he, not especially pleased at any sort of understanding between the young lady before him and Howard.

"Anything you·like."

"I should like nothing so much as—"

"As what?"

"No; upon reflection I don't think I dare mention it," Granton said coolly, looking at her with an expression in his big brown eyes which made her flush in spite of herself.

"Don't be impudent," she replied. "That is my province."

"Time!" called the umpire, a little later. "Howard and Granton, concluding set."

"Wish me luck," Granton murmured, bending toward Betty as he rose.

"I'm sure I do, for my own sake," she responded, with an ambiguity he afterward had reason to understand.

"What shall I do if Mr. Howard beats him?" Betty said to George and Dora, as the set began. "There'd be no fun playing him instead of Mr. Granton."

"Oh, Howard hasn't the ghost of a chance," George responded reassuringly. "You are all right, Bet, if you don't get nervous."

But Betty did get nervous. The color came and went in her cheeks almost as swiftly as the flying balls were thrown, whose skilful service and returns soon proved Snow to be right in asserting that Howard had no chance against his antagonist.

"Oh, George," she whispered, in an agony of apprehension, "can I do it? Won't he beat me? It would be too horrible to challenge him and then fail!"

"Do it?" retorted her cousin; "of course you can do it! See that short serve. That's what's breaking Howard up: it's easy for you to return if you'll run up to it. His swift service does n't begin to be as good as yours."

"Love set," called the scorer; and as Betty looked at the supple, muscular figure of Nat Granton while the players exchanged courts, her fears almost overcame her resolve.

"My heart is thumping against my very boot-heels, Dolly." she confided to her friend. "It's no sort of use."

"Are you going to give up?" demanded Dora curiously, and perhaps a little tauntingly.

"Give up!" cried Mistress Mork stoutly. "Do I ever give up? I'll die first! But I do wish he would n't get so many love games! It's dreadfully discouraging."

Granton was, in truth, having everything his own way. Howard, although a good player, had somehow lost his coolness, and

was soon demoralized by a peculiar short,
cutting service, of which his opponent had
complete mastery, and which he was unable
to return. His play became wild and uneven, and the contest was quickly decided
against him.

The master of ceremonies came forward
with the announcement that the prize racquet belonged to Mr. Nathaniel Granton, but
that, according to the provisions of the tournament, any person had now a right to challenge the winner to play for the prize, by the
best two games in three.

There was a rustle, and then a pause, as
many eyes were turned toward George Snow,
who had won in the Newport games the
summer before. But that gentleman sat
quiet in his place, a smile of amusement
stealing over his comely features as Dora
said, in the most tragic of whispers,—

" Oh, Betty, how can you? "

But Betty, her head thrown a trifle back,
and the color flaming hotly into her face,
rose with a charming mixture of dignity
and shyness, and walked, before them all,
straight up to the judges.

" I challenge the winner to a match," she
said, steadily enough, although she confided
to Dora afterward that she felt as if every

word had to be dragged out by main force. "I should like five minutes to change my dress."

Granton uttered a low, sharp whistle, and doffed his cap.

"All right," the master of ceremonies returned. "Be as quick as you can."

"I'll not keep you waiting long," she assured him, and turned to beckon Dora to her.

As the two girls disappeared into the hotel, the bustle and chatter began again with renewed vigor, and swelled and buzzed in the liveliest fashion. Here was a genuine sensation for Maugus. Betty was too lovely and too great a favorite with the men wholly to escape the censure of the young ladies, who now had a string of pretty things to say of her boldness and presumption. But the gentlemen rallied to a man in her support, and, by the time she reappeared, public opinion, as represented by the spectators of the tournament, if not wholly in her favor, was so in outward expression.

She was dressed in a dark-blue jersey of silk, which fitted her in that perfect combination only possible with a faultless figure and an irreproachable jersey; and below that a skirt of navy-blue flannel fell in straight plaits to her ankles, where one

caught, as she moved, occasional glimpses
of a crimson stocking, the exact shade of
her flat sash and of the close wing-tip in her
trig little blue silk cap. There was nothing
of the nature of tags and ends about her
costume. Her hair was closely coiled, and
even her ear-rings had been removed. The
crimson handkerchief about her white throat
was fastened into its place so securely as
scarcely to be less smooth when the playing
was over than when the first game began.

She was very sober, — so grave, indeed,
that George went over to her just as she
took her place, to say some absurd thing to
make her laugh.

"Don't be nervous," he added, having
succeeded in his object so far as to call a
fleeting smile to her face. "And don't
look as if assisting at your own obsequies.
You are all right, if you 'll only think so."

"Will she do it?" Dora asked anxiously,
as he took his seat again.

"I'm sure I don't know," he answered.
"I've told her she will, and I hope so; but
it is n't going to be so easy."

They talked of that tennis tournament for
many a long day in Maugus. Opinion was
divided at first as to the probable result.
There was a quiet concentration in Betty's

manner which soon began to awake confidence in her ultimate success, although at first she lost. Even the most envious of the girls soon found themselves applauding every lucky hit she made; and Betty, whose senses were keenly alive that day, felt the stimulating consciousness that the general sympathy was with her. She threw her whole soul into her playing, every point she lost arousing her to new exertions.

" By Jove! Dora," George said, " Granton's bound to get a lesson. Betty's blood is getting up. I'm convinced now that she'll win, and I'll bet you the gloves that she beats him a love set before she's done."

Dora was too excited to answer him. She hoped he might be right, but just now Betty was losing. She had been beaten three games out of five, and the present one, on Granton's service, was going hard against her. Granton was harassing her with his short cut, which fell before her racquet reached it nearly every time.

" What's got into her?" George muttered uneasily. " Ah, that was better. Good return."

And he led the hand-clapping which greeted the difficult stroke by which Betty brought the score up to deuce. The game went against her, however, and soon after, the set.

" I 'll do it, George," Betty said under her breath, as she passed him in changing courts. " Don't be discouraged. The Mork blood is up."

" It 's all on his cuts, Bet. Run up to them. Watch his service, and you can tell when they are coming. Nat could never serve a decent swift ball."

Betty nodded and went on to her place.

" Play ! " called Granton.

Watching him, his opponent noticed him throw his head back, and remembered his telling her that he always betrayed his cutting. She ran toward the net as the ball came down, and returned it like a cannonball.

" She 's got it ! " cried Snow, with great glee, in his excitement calling so loudly that both the players heard him. " She 's all right now. Oh, that 's beautiful ! "

Granton tried a couple of swift balls and faulted them both.

" Love ; thirty," called the scorer.

Another cut ; again cleverly intercepted ; then a fault and an easy, round-hand service.

" Love ; game."

The applause was really quite tremendous.

"They are all against me," Granton observed to Betty, handing her the balls over the net and laughing rather ruefully. "Public opinion would be positively outraged if you should fail."

"I've no intention of failing, thank you," she returned, with spirit; and away she swept to her position. "Play!"

Granton was himself on his mettle, yet he did not play his best. He could not fully recover from his surprise at the style of his adversary's play. The swiftness of her service and returns was so different from what was expected of a girl that he was scarcely on his guard against it up to the very end. He felt the sympathy of the spectators, too, to be against him, and this was not without its influence. He lost the set, and with it, by an unfortunate chance, his good nature.

"Sets, one all," the scorer announced; and something in the saucy toss of Betty's lovely head, as, flushed and panting, she stood talking with George and Dora, jarred upon her lover's nerves with sudden irritation. An unreasonable madness took possession of him. How much was wounded vanity, it might not be easy to say; but under the circumstances, with all his mates grinning at his failure, it was not at all strange that

his feelings were not wholly placid. His
play in the third and decisive set became
rash and excited. He lost his head a little,
and before he fairly knew how it happened
the score was called on Betty's service: —

"Games; five, love."

"Good!" was George Snow's comment.
"I told you she'd beat a love set before
she was done. — Oh, keep your head, Bet!"

Betty delivered a ball swift as a bullet
and just clearing the net.

"Fifteen; love."

A fault, and then another swift ball, which
skimmed like a swallow over the net and
struck the ground only to cling to it in a
swift roll.

"Thirty; love."

The next ball was beaten back and forth
until Granton dashed it to the ground at
Betty's very feet.

"Thirty; fifteen."

The excitement was at its height. Even
those who did not appreciate the finer points
of the play caught the interest and somehow
understood pretty accurately how matters
stood, and were as earnest as the rest.
Small-talk was forgotten, heads were craned
forward, and all eyes were fixed upon the
players. Betty grasped her racquet by

the extreme end of its handle, and held the ball as high above her head as she could reach.

" Play ! "

She struck it with all her force.

" Forty; fifteen," was the scorer's call; and Nat Granton understood that only one stroke lay between him and defeat by a love set.

George Snow deliberately turned away his face.

" I never supposed I could be such a consummate fool," he said afterward, " but I positively could not look at your last service, Bet. I felt as if the whole universe were at stake."

As for the player, she was fairly pale with excitement; but her head was clear and her hand steady. She paused an instant, poising her racquet. She observed that Granton stood near the middle of his court. With a quick step she moved to the very outer corner of her own and sent a swift ball sharply under her opponent's left hand.

" Game; love set," called the scorer. " Sets two to one in favor of Miss Mork."

And, amid what for Maugus was a really astonishing round of applause, Betty, flushed but triumphant, walked to the net to shake hands with her vanquished lover.

V.

IT was astonishing how humble and for-
giving her victory made Mistress Betty. She
was troubled with the fear that she had been
unmaidenly, that she had hurt Granton's feelings and alienated his friendship forever, with
a dozen more scruples quite as absurd and
irrational.

She escaped as quickly as possible from
her friends and their congratulations, and
hurried to her room on the pretext of dressing for supper. There she cooled her hot
cheeks, burning with exercise and excitement,
and looking ruefully at her image in the
mirror, shook her head reproachfully at the
counterfeit presentment as at one who had
beguiled her into misdoing.

After supper she was sitting rather gloomily
in a retired corner of the piazza, when the
defeated Granton approached. The reaction
from the afternoon's excitement had rendered
the young lady's spirit rather subdued, but
she rallied at sight of the new-comer.

" Good-evening," he said. " Were you enjoying the sweets of victory? "

" I was enjoying the sweets of solitude,"
she returned, a little pointedly.

Granton laughed.

" I suppose," he remarked, taking a vacant chair near her, " that I need not apologize for my ill-judged remarks some time since about girls and tennis. My afternoon's punishment ought to pass as a sufficient expiation."

" Expiation is always a matter of feeling."

" Oh, as to that, I felt I had enough, I assure you," he laughed. " It may not be gallant to say so, but it was really horrible to be beaten out of my boots by a lady in broad daylight, in face of all Maugus assembled."

Betty was silent. The remorseful feeling rose again in her breast. Granton spoke lightly enough, but she wondered if she had not humiliated him terribly. She played nervously with her fan, hardly knowing how to phrase it, yet longing to offer something in the way of apology.

" I hope," she began, " I hope — "

Nat regarded her closely in the fading light as she hesitated, and by some happy inspiration divined her softened mood. He noted the downcast eyes and troubled face. Without fully comprehending her mental state, he yet found courage to move a trifle nearer.

" Yes? " he queried, laying his fingers upon the arm of her chair.

Betty looked at the hand which had ap-

9

proached so near, and a sudden trepidation thrilled her. She opened and closed her fan nervously, but made no attempt to finish her broken sentence.

"Betty," her lover said, leaning forward, "now I am in the dust at your feet, you must at least let me speak. You 've kept out of my way so for the last two or three weeks that I was afraid you disliked me; but now I understand where you have been. You know how much I care for you."

Still she did not raise her eyes.

"Don't you care for me?" he pleaded. "I 've been in love with you all summer. You must have known it."

He paused again, yet she did not answer, though a great tide of joy thrilled her whole being. Her lover seized both her hands and bent down until his cheek almost touched hers.

"Will you marry me, Betty?"

All her wilfulness and sauciness flashed in her eyes as she lifted her glance at last to his and answered.

"I would n't if I had n't beaten this afternoon."

With which implied consent he seemed perfectly satisfied.

Interlude Third.

———•———

MRS. FRUFFLES IS AT HOME.

MRS. FRUFFLES IS AT HOME.

In answer to the announcement that Mrs. Stephen Morgan _Fruffles will, on the afternoon of January 27, be at home from four to seven, all the world — with the exception of her husband, who keeps significantly out of the house, and at his club finds such solace as is possible under the circumstances — has assembled to celebrate that rare and exciting event.

The parlors are thronged almost to suffocation; the air is warm, and laden with a hundred odors, which combine to make it well-nigh unbreathable; the constant babble of conversation goes on with the steady click-clack of a mill-wheel, and several hundred people persistently talk without saying anything whatever.

Mrs. Chumley Jones is there, in a most effective costume of garnet plush, adorned with some sort of long-haired black fur. She is conscious of being perfectly well dressed, of being the best-known woman in the parlors, and most of all is she now, as always, conscious of being the one and only Mrs. Chumley Jones. Soothed and sustained by an unfaltering trust in all these good things, she moves slowly through the rooms, or stands at some convenient coign of vantage, dropping a word to this one and to that, with just the right differences of manner fitted to the degrees of the people whom she addresses.

"My dear Mrs. Fruffles," she remarks to the hostess, " you do always have such enchanting receptions ! "

"Oh, thank you, dear Mrs. Jones," responds the other, fully aware what is expected of her ; " I wish I could begin to have anything so charming as your Fridays."

"Oh, so kind of you to say so," murmurs Mrs. Jones, with the expressive shake of the head proper to the sentiment and the occasion.

Then she passes on to her duty elsewhere.

"How do you do, Mrs. Jones?" the voice of Ferdinand Maunder·says at her side. " Isn't it a lovely day? It is really like a Roman winter; don't you think so?"

"Yes, it really is, Mr. Maunder."

"Yes, that's what I've been saying to myself all day."

"It is so much nicer of you to say it to me."

"Oh, Mrs. Jones, you are always so clever at turning things."

They smile at each other with perfect and well-bred inanity for a second, and then Fred Lasceet slips in between them.

"How do you do, Mrs. Jones?"

"Oh, how do you do, Mr. Lasceet? It is ever so long since I have seen you."

"So good of you to think it long. I am sure it seems an age to me."

Mr. Maunder having meanwhile glided through the crowd with an eel-like elusiveness, Mrs. Chumley Jones is left with a remark upon which to form her conversation for the afternoon.

"We have had such a strange winter; don't you think so, Mr. Lasceet? It is really like a Roman winter."

"It really is; though I should n't have thought of it. You are always so clever in thinking of things, Mrs. Jones."

"You are a sad flatterer, Mr. Lasceet."

Mr. Lasceet endeavors to look very sly and cunning, and while he gives his mind to this endeavor another slips into his place.

"How do you do, Mrs. Jones?" says Percival Drummond.

"Oh, how do you do, Mr. Drummond? I have n't seen you for ever so long."

Mr. Lasceet melts into the swaying background, and is seen no more.

"It really is not nice of you to say so, Mrs. Jones," is Mr. Drummond's response, "when I took you in to dinner at Mrs. Tiger's night before last."

"Oh, dear me; how stupid of me! I really fear I am losing my mind. It is the weather, I think. It is so like a Roman winter, don't you think?"

"Yes, it is a little."

"Oh, ever so much. How do you do, dear Mrs. Gray? I am delighted to see you. I was just saying to Mr. Drummond that it seems to me that our winter this year is so much like a Roman winter. Did you ever think of it?"

"Oh, my dear, I have thought of nothing else all winter. Why, it is just such a day as it was one afternoon two years ago when I was in Rome."

"Were you in Rome year before last?" Mr. Drummond inquires, with the air of one to whom the answer of the question is of the most vital importance, although he asks only for the sake of being silent no longer.

"Yes, we went in October and stayed until March. You remember, Mrs. Jones, that we dined with you the very day before we sailed."

"Why, yes, so you did. I had forgotten all about it. Are you going?"

"Yes, I really must go. I have three places more to call before I go home, and we are going out to dinner."

"I shall see you if you dine at the Muchmen's."

"Oh, are you to be there? How lovely."

"I hope to take one of you in," Mr. Drummond says, with a smile of the most brilliant vacuity.

"Are you to be there, too? Why, it will be quite a reunion. *Au revoir.*"

The crowd swallows Mrs. Gray, and at the same

moment Mr. Drummond is seized upon by a sharp-looking elderly female, who drags him off as if she were conveying him into some sly corner where she may devour him undisturbed. Mrs. Jones turns to move toward the other parlor.

At that moment she is accosted by a lady of an appearance so airy, both as regards dress and manner, as to suggest that she is a mislaid member of some ballet troupe.

" Why, how do you do? " she cried, with a vivacity quite in keeping with her appearance. " My dear Mrs. Jones, I have n't seen you since I got back from Europe."

" Why, Susie Throgmorton, is it really you? I did n't know you were home."

" 'That shows what an unimportant person I am."

" Oh, I knew you came home from Europe, but I thought you were still in New York."

" Oh, I only went on to see Aunt Dinah for a couple of days. I got caught in the most awful storm you ever saw."

" But the winter," Mrs. Chumley Jones observes, with an air of freshness and conviction which is something beautiful to see, " has been as mild as a Roman winter most of the time."

" Yes, it has been like a Roman winter."

The crowd separates them and they go their several ways, each repeating that it is like a Roman winter; but meanwhile the same observation is

being scattered broadcast by Mr. Maunder, Mr.
Lasceet, and Mr. Drummond, so that, although
there are a good many people in the room, they
are in a fair way of being all informed that the
winter strongly resembles that of Rome ; a statement which, if true, may be regarded as of the
highest importance.   ·

It is not until, entering the tea room, Mrs.
Chumley Jones encounters Mrs. Quagget, who
talks more rapidly than any other known woman,
that she has anybody take the words out of her
mouth ; but before she can tell Mrs. Quagget that
it is like a Roman winter, Mrs. Quagget has imparted that interesting information to her.   It is
all one, however, since something has been said
by one of them ; and Mrs. Chumley Jones is not
in the least disconcerted.   She still clings to the
convenient remark, as she did not take the trouble
to bring one with her, and this one suits her purpose admirably.

"My dear Miss Tarrart," she exclaims, as she
comes upon a wintry young lady of advanced stages
of maturity, "how do you do?   I have n't seen you
for an age."

"Why, how do you do, Mrs. Jones?" is the
response, delivered in a manner so emphatic as to
convey the impression that the reason why Miss
Tarrart is so odd-looking is because she has put so
much energy into her greetings of her friends.
"I am enchanted to see you.   When do you go

abroad? I am sure one might almost think they were abroad in this weather. It is so — "

"Yes," Mrs. Jones interposes, taking the words out of her mouth; "I was just saying to Mrs. Quagget that this is really quite like a Roman winter; don't you think so?"

"Yes, it is," Miss Tarrart answers, with the air of one who has been beaten by unfair means. "It is like a Roman winter."

"Why don't you come and see me, Miss Tarrart? It really is not kind of you to stay away so long."

"I am coming very soon; and you must come and see me."

"Oh, yes; I am coming. Do you know which way Mrs. Fruffles is? I really must go."

"She is in the other room."

"Well, good-bye, dear."

"Good-bye."

The two separate, each thinking how fast the other is growing old. Mrs. Chumley Jones, feeling that she has now done her whole duty, does not even take the trouble any more to tell people that the winter is like a Roman one. She merely makes her way to the hostess.

"Good-bye," she says. "One always has such lovely times at your house, Mrs. Fruffles."

"Oh, it is so kind of you to say so, when your Fridays are so much pleasanter."

"It is so kind of you to say so, my dear Mrs.

Fruffles ; but I am sorry to say that I cannot agree
with you."

" It is the weather partly," the hostess observes ;
" so many people have said to me this afternoon
that it seems like a Roman winter."

"Yes, I was just thinking of that very thing.
Well, good-bye, my dear.   Be sure and come in on
Friday."

" Oh, I would n't miss it for anything."

" Good-bye."

" Good-bye."

And as far as Mrs. Chumley Jones is concerned,
Mrs. Stephen Morgan Fruffles ceases to be " At
Home."

Cale the Fourth.

JOHN VANTINE.

JOHN VANTINE.

THE relation of so improbable a story as the following is to be justified only by its truth. The hero is a New York lawyer, sufficiently well known to render the mention of his name, were it allowable to give it, an ample guarantee for the entire trustworthiness of any statement he might make; and it is perhaps to be regretted that his invincible — albeit natural — dislike of publicity prevents the production of evidence which would at least establish the fact that his own belief in the appearances by which he was visited is complete and sincere.

Mr. Vantine, although a handsome and intellectual-looking man, is by no means a person whose appearance would in any way single him out as likely to be the hero of marvellous adventures. He is neither especially imaginative nor credulous. He is simply a clear-headed and shrewd business man, such as are nourished in the atmosphere of New York, of all places in the wide world, perhaps, the one least likely to nourish fancy or belief in the unseen. To see him going steadily about his affairs down town, it is hardly probable that any observer, however keen, would look on him as the probable object of remarkable hallucinations, or of experiences so far from the ordinary course of human life, as sure to be classed as such by ninety-nine men out of a hundred.

Yet John Vantine, of whom most of his acquaintances would have said that he was a commonplace man of business, lived for years a double life, into which he did not venture to initiate even his wife, with whom he lived on terms of the warmest sympathy and closest confidence.

It was on the morning of his wedding-day that certain impressions, which in a vague shape had for years haunted him, first took form so definite that he could not but think of them as something having a tangibility of their own, different though it was from that of the ordinary things which surround common human life. He was married at the home of his bride, a pretty village in western Massachusetts. There being no hotel of even decent comfort in the place, Vantine had passed the night at the inn of a town half a dozen miles away, whence he drove over in the dewy June morning to the scene of his marriage.

As he passed along between the fields starred with daisies, reflecting in blissful mood upon the beauty of the day and the happiness it brought to him, his horse came suddenly and without warning to a standstill. John instinctively gathered up the reins to start the animal, when to his unspeakable amazement he perceived a man in an Eastern dress of great splendor standing beside the open carriage. His robes were of the richest stuffs, while jewels sparkled from every part of his attire. He was standing apparently upon a small rug, a circumstance which at the moment impressed Vantine more than his mysterious presence. The stranger saluted the young man with the most profound obeisances, and it was only after repeated genuflections that he spoke. When he did address Vantine, it was in a language of which the latter did not even know the name, although in some astonishing way he still comprehended what was.said.

"Great Master," the stranger greeted him, "will you receive an embassy to congratulate you on your nuptials?"

Of course I cannot pretend here or elsewhere to give the exact words in which my friend was addressed. It was some years before he confided the story to me, and although I have endeavored to set the words down exactly as he gave them, it must be borne in mind that he made no attempt at literal verbal accuracy.

That a young man who had been nourished amid the hard commonplaces of New York life should be astounded by an address of this sort was only natural. That Vantine did not lose his head altogether was probably due to certain vague and premonitory experiences which he never defined very clearly, alluding to them as " passing fancies," " nebulous impressions," and by other phrases too general to convey exact meaning to my mind. On the present occasion, however, beyond a rather prolonged silence before he answered his interlocutor, he seems to have behaved much as might a man stopped on the street by an ordinary acquaintance. When he spoke, he simply and laconically answered " Yes ; " and, as he did so, he swept with his eye the wide horizon which the nature of the country laid open to him, perceiving nowhere sign of anything unusual.

Scarcely, however, had the monosyllable left his lips when he saw upon the woodside an enormous oriental rug cover the green-

sward, and instantly upon it stood a numerous company, dressed in the most splendid
robes, saluting, and uttering stately but most
enthusiastic congratulations. In this, as in all
other instances in which my friend has seen
figures, the lower portions have appeared
first.

John sat in dignified and very probably
half-stupefied silence during this extraordinary scene, and suddenly, without warning,
the whole pageant vanished into the limbo
from which it had come. He was once more
alone upon a country road, in the bright sunshine of a June forenoon. It was his wedding morning, and, the vision or whatever it
might properly be called having vanished,
there was obviously nothing to do but to
drive on and be married, — a course of action
which he carried out to the letter.

I have fancied, although it is a point upon
which I am doubtful, that John made some
beginning of a confidence to his bride during
the honeymoon of this extraordinary occur-
rence, and that the levity with which she
received his first suggestions prevented his
going further in his disclosures. The reason
is, however, of no great consequence, but at
least the fact is that he did not tell her. He
gave a good deal of thought to the matter,

corresponded with the Psychical Society, of London, not relating his own experience, but endeavoring to learn of a parallel case. He had, too, some communication with the Theosophical Society, of London, and even with the parent society, of Madras; and he at one time contemplated making a confidant of Madame Blavatsky, concerning whom, at that time, the European papers were full of marvellous tales.

He does not seem, so far as I am able to gather from what he has told me, to have hit upon any theory which afforded him a clue to the mystery of his own case; and just as he had made up his mind that the whole was a mere optical delusion, he had a second visitation.

He was in a Fifth Avenue car on the elevated road, returning home at night. The car was compactly filled, but before him, as he sat facing the middle of the car, was an open space, two or three feet square. Looking up, as the train started after stopping at the Twenty-third street station, John saw standing before him the same oriental figure which had greeted him on his wedding day. The stranger's face beamed with joy, and he scarcely waited to finish his profound salutation before exclaiming, "It is a propitious hour, Great Master. The young prince is a pearl beyond price."

Vantine's first instinct was to look at his neighbors, to see whether they too beheld the apparition, if apparition it were. The man on his right was looking up from his newspaper with the air of one who had heard the strange words and wished to discover whence they came. The man on the left was gazing at Vantine with an expression of bewildered curiosity. John turned his eyes again to the spot where his strange visitor had been.

The place was vacant.

My friend, in relating this, blamed himself severely that he had allowed a natural diffidence to prevent his asking his neighbors whether they had seen the "Great Mogul," as he began facetiously to dub the phantom in his thoughts. "But," he added, "nobody likes to be taken for a raving idiot, even by a stranger. They certainly looked as if they had seen the figure, but I could n't make up my mind to ask."

Reaching home, John found that his wife had been prematurely but safely delivered of a lusty son. The messenger sent to his office had missed him, and at the time of the appearance in the car, he declares that he was not consciously even thinking of his wife's condition at all.

When he had time to collect his thoughts after this second visitation, Vantine came firmly to the resolution that if he were ever favored with a third sight of the "Great Mogul," he would at least endeavor to discover whether the phantom were appreciable by the sense of touch. He read much about "astral appearances," and a good many more things of the sort, of which my own knowledge is too limited to permit my writing at all. He formed a hundred theories, and he began to get somewhat confused, to use his own expression, in regard to his identity. He was half convinced that by some misworking of the law of re-incarnation, the spirit of some Eastern potentate had been put into his body.

"Or," said he, with a whimsicality which was evidently deeply tinctured with a serious feeling, "that I had got into somebody's else body. If I had known any possible way of stopping the thing, it would n't have been so bad; but to have the 'Great Mogul' pop up like a jack-in-a-box, without any warning, was taking me at a disadvantage that I think decidedly unfair."

Not to lengthen unnecessarily a simple

story, the speculations and investigations of Vantine may be passed over, and the narrative confined to the bare facts.

It was when John's boy was about two months old that the embassy which had greeted John upon his wedding morning, or one closely resembling it, put in an appearance in honor of the child's birth. The child and its mother were taking their first drive, and Vantine came home to luncheon rather earlier than usual, to find them out. He went into the library, but had scarcely closed the door behind him, when the whole gorgeous company of his wedding morning were before him, and so real did they seem to him that John entirely forgot his intention of grasping the "Great Mogul" by the arm, to convince himself of the reality of that personage. The company overflowed with congratulations, rather florid to my friend's occidentally trained taste, but doubtless poetical in the extreme from an oriental point of view. Vantine was afterward amused and a little surprised to remember how much as a matter of course he took the adulation offered him, and the ease with which he played the rôle of "Great Master."

But suddenly he became so thoroughly amazed that all power of speech or motion

seemed to forsake him. In the arms of the
" Great Mogul" he perceived his baby boy,
or an image that seemed to be the child, and .
to the babe the brilliant company were kneel-
ing and swearing fealty. The whole ceremony occupied about half an hour, at the end
of which time Vantine found himself once
more alone, and upon going downstairs he
met his wife and the nurse with the baby returning from their drive.

"He 's slept like a dormouse," Mrs. Vantine said, in answer to her husband's inquiry.
"I tried to rouse him once, but he would n't
wake. I was half frightened, but he seems
all right now."

As they entered the parlor the maid came
to inquire if Mr. Vantine had brought company to luncheon, as she had heard voices
in the library, — a circumstance which proved
that the sound of the voices of his ghostly vis-
itors was audible to other ears than his own.

John vainly wished that the baby, healthy,
awake and cooing now, could tell whether
dreams or strange experiences had troubled
its sleep while its father had seen its image;
but that is a point upon which he has never
received enlightenment.

It was one winter night when the baby was
six months old that the " Great Mogul"

presented himself again. My friend had been taking a bath, and was dressing for bed when the figure of his visions appeared, and with every mark of terror and consternation prostrated itself at his feet.

" Great Master," it gasped in the usual formula, " pardon your slave's intrusion. The enemy are upon us. They — "

With this sentence still unfinished, the vision faded away in an instant, as if some unforeseen catastrophe in whatever region it came from had suddenly recalled the eidolon, or projected presence, or whatever the thing might be.

More confounded and disturbed than ever, my friend retired to bed, but he was too much excited to sleep. He had much the feeling that one fancies a prince to have over whose heritage distant armies are contending, while he in forced inaction awaits the result. No clue had been given which enabled him to reach a solution of the mystery that involved him, and nothing further transpired during the night to render matters any plainer.

On the following afternoon he was obliged to start for Boston on business. As he was elbowing his way through the crowd in the Grand Central station, he heard at his ear the

well known voice of the "Great Mogul,"
speaking as usual in the unknown tongue
which Vantine understood, yet the identity of
which he had never established.   There was
no visible appearance this time, and the voice,
although distinctly audible, seemed to come
from a great distance.

" Great Master," the voice said, " they are
beheading me.   All is lost."

" It would be some comfort," John Vantine
said, rather irritably, when he confided this
strange story to me, " to know what was lost.
It would have been uncommonly civil of the
' Great Mogul' to be a little more definite in
his information.   If the poor fellow lost his
head in my service I am profoundly grateful,
of course; but precious little good does it do
me.   Do you think the Psychical Society
would undertake the job of discovering in
what part of the universe I am rightfully
dubbed the Great Master and that young
rascal in the nursery is a prince!   Unless
they can do something, I'm afraid I shall
be a half-starved New York lawyer to the
end of the chapter."

To which I had nothing satisfactory to
answer.

Interlude Fourth.

THE RADIATOR.

THE RADIATOR.

A STUDY IN THE MODERN STYLE OF COLLOQUIAL
FICTION.

[*Scene, the chamber of Mr. and Mrs. Ellston, in an apartment hotel. Time, three* A. M. *The silence of the night is unbroken, save by the regular breathing of the sleepers, until suddenly, from the steam radiator, bursts a sound like the discharge of a battery of forty-pound guns.*]

Mrs. E. (*springing up in bed*) Oh! eh? what is that?

[*Her husband moves uneasily in his sleep, but does not reply. The noise of the sledge-hammer score of the "Anvil Chorus" rings out from the radiator.*]

Mrs. E. George! George! Something is going to happen! Do wake up, or we shall be murdered in our sleep!

Mr. E. (*with mingled ferocity and amusement*) There is small danger of anybody's being murdered in his sleep, my dear, where you are. It's only that confounded radiator; it's always making some sort of an infernal tumult. It can't do any harm.

Mrs. E. But it will wake baby.

Mr. E. Well, if it does, the nurse can get him to sleep again, I suppose.

[*From the room adjoining is heard a clattering din, as if all the kettles and pans in the house were being thrown violently across the floor.*]

Mrs. E. There! The nursery radiator has begun. I must go and get baby.

Mr. E. Let baby alone. If the youngster will sleep, for heaven's sake let him. The steam-pipes make noise enough for this time of night, one would think, without your taking the trouble to wake baby.

Mrs. E. (*with volumes of reproach in her tone*) Your own little baby! You never loved him as his mother does.

[*The disturbances now assume the likeness to a thoroughly inebriated drum corps practising upon sheet-iron air-tight stoves.*]

Mr. E. Of all unendurable rackets —

[*A sudden and sharp boom interrupts him. Mrs. Ellston screams, while her husband indulges in language which, although somewhat inexcusably forcible, is yet to be regarded as not unnatural under the circumstances.*]

Mrs. E. Oh, George, don't swear. It always seems so much worse to swear in danger; like tempting Providence; and I know there's going to be an explosion!

Mr. E. (*severely*) Don't talk nonsense! The engineer has gone to sleep and left the drafts open, that's all. Don't be so absurd.

[*There is another fusillade from the radiator, reinforced by the reverberations from the nursery, where a regiment of artillery seem to have begun target practice.*]

Mrs. E. I *will* go and get my baby ! I know — Oh, George, just hear it crash ! Do get up and put the screen in front of it ; that may turn off the pieces so they won't come this way.

Mr. E. (*scornfully*) Pieces of what? Noise?

Mrs. E. How can you make fun? If the engineer has gone to sleep, he 's sure to blow up the whole hotel. I 'm going to get up and dress myself, and take baby over to mother's !

Mr. E. (*with calm but cutting irony*) At three o'clock in the morning? Shall you walk, or call a carriage?

Mrs. E. (*beginning to sob in a dry and perfunctory fashion*) Oh, you are too cruel ! You are perfectly heartless. I wonder you don't take that dear little innocent baby and hold him between you and the radiator for a shield.

Mr. E. That might be a good scheme, my dear, only the little beggar would probably howl so that I have n't really the moral courage to wake him.

[*The indignant reply of Mrs. Ellston is lost in the confused sound of the brays of a drove of brazen donkeys, which appear to be disporting themselves in the radiator. The noise of mighty rushing waters, the clanking of chains, the din of a political convention, the characteristic disturbances of a hundred factories and machine-shops, with the deafening whirr of all the elevated railways in the universe follow in turn.*]

Mrs. E. I *will* go and get my baby, and I will

go to mother's; and, what is more, we will never, never come back!

Mr. E. Oh, just as you please about going, my dear; only you know that if you desert my bed and board, the law gives the boy to me.

Mrs. E. I don't *believe* it's any such thing; and if it is, it is because men made the law. Women would n't take a baby away from its mother.

Mr. E. Have what theories you choose, my dear; only please let me get a few crumbs of sleep, now the radiator has had the mercy to subside.

Mrs. E. You are a brute, and I won't ever speak to you again!

[*She firmly assumes a stony silence, and the radiator, after a few concluding ejaculations and metallic objurgations, also relapses into comparative stillness. Mr. Ellston's breathing begins to give strong indications that slumber has re-descended upon his weary frame.*]

Mrs. E. (*starting up with the inspiration of an entirely new and startling idea*) George! George! George!

Mr. E. (*with less good humor than might be desired*) Eh?

Mrs. E. Was n't it wonderful for baby to sleep through it all?

Mr. E. (*drowsily*) Yes; droll little beggar. His mother was n't in the nursery to wake him, though.

Mrs. E. You don't suppose there is anything the matter with him? George! George, I say! you don't suppose the reason he sleeps so soundly is because he's sick?

[*To this conundrum Mr. Ellston offers no solution, and equally passes in silence queries in regard to the probability of the nurse's being awake, alive, well-disposed, and able to take care of baby in case of emergency. Mrs. Ellston sighs with the desperation of long-suffering anguish, and once more stillness reigns in the chamber. The lady again arouses herself, however, from an apparently sound nap to ask, in penetrating tones, —*]

"George, *do* you think it will begin all over again?"

(*To which her brutal worser half grumbles out the reply*) "No! and that's where it is more endurable than a woman."

[*At which the radiator gives a chuckle so apt as to suggest the possession of a sinister consciousness on the part of that noisy instrument of torture. Mrs. Ellston groans, with the discouraged conviction that she is but one against two, and upon this theory at length consents to resume her interrupted slumbers.*]

Tale the Fifth.

MÈRE MARCHETTE.

MÈRE MARCHETTE.

I.

IT was half-past eleven of a hot July day in Paris. The sunlight lay over the whole city and shone nowhere more strongly than upon the great hospital of the Salpêtrière. The hush of noon brooded over all the place. Nobody was stirring unless forced to activity by some pressing duty. In the long white wards the patients were asleep or lying quiet in exhaustion under the burning fervor of the summer heat.

Down one of the corridors, where it seemed refreshingly cool after the warmth of the outer air from which he had come, a young man was passing. His step, though rapid, had the noiseless quality which bespeaks familiarity with the sick-room and the hospital. His figure was compact and nervous, his glance clear and keen. Dr. Jean Lommel was one of the house physicians of the

Salpêtrière, although that he was not now making his regular rounds was evident from the fact that entering a certain ward he passed quickly to a bed near the middle of it without stopping at any of the others.

On the bed lay an old woman. Her face was one which showed great strength of character. It was of a marked peasant type, and for all its innumerable wrinkles, its sunken temples, the coarse texture of its skin, and the shrunken lips which showed the lack of teeth behind them, it was full of a nobility and kindliness which no ravages of time or disease could wholly hide. The hair that straggled in thin locks from beneath the white cap was hardly less snowy than the lawn which covered it; and when the patient opened her sunken eyes, as the doctor stopped beside the bed, they were bright and shining with a lustre which was not all either fever or anxiety. Her glance was one of intense and pitiful inquiry. The young man touched her white hair with the tips of his long, fine fingers in a pitying caress before he took hold of the withered wrist, shrunken and marked with blue veins, that lay outside the coverlid.

"In an hour, Mère Marchette," he said, answering her look — " in an hour he will be here; keep up a good heart. You do not suffer?"

The old woman feebly shook her head. The ghost of a smile, faint but full of happiness, shone on her face. She did not speak, but she thanked him with a look before she closed her eyes and lay motionless as before he had come.

The young man looked at her a moment, an expression of pity in his brown eyes; then with a sigh he turned away and moved softly down the ward again. By the door he encountered one of the nurses, who had risen and come forward to speak with him.

" Will she live, M. Lommel? "

" Yes," the doctor answered. " She has given all her energies for days to keeping alive till her grandson gets here. It is very singular," he went on, in a voice of low distinctness that could have been acquired only in sick-rooms, " how her instinct has taught her to save her strength. She neither moves nor speaks; she simply lives."

" She has been that way," the nurse returned, "ever since we told her that Pierre was coming. Will he be here by twelve? "

" Not till half-past twelve," Dr. Lommel replied. " I will return before then."

And he went out into the hot sunshine.

II.

EVERYBODY connected with the ward of the Salpêtrière wherein she was had a kindly feeling for poor old Mère Marchette. The doctors and the nurses could not have been more kind or more tender had she been of their own blood. She was one of those who always win affection. She was so patient, so simple, so kindly. She was a peasant woman from Normandy, who had in her old age drifted to Paris with her grandson Pierre, a lad of sixteen years. All the rest of the family were dead. Pierre's father had been a soldier, and it was with the hope of securing a pension for the son that Mère Marchette had left her home and the life in Normandy she loved, to throw herself into Paris as into the sea. The dead soldier, however, had been mustered out before the malarial fever, contracted in the swamps of the Landes, had developed itself, and the pension could not be obtained. The disappointment was a bitter one, made worse by the fact that Mère Marchette had been told by one and another that the claim would have been granted had the case been properly managed. The poor old creature could not escape a feeling of self-blame in thinking that it was her want of keenness which had deprived Pierre of his pension. Her grandson for her represented the world, and to him she devoted all her energies. She toiled for him, and watched and suffered with that unselfish egotism possible only to the old and lonely.

Fortunately Pierre was a good lad, who returned his grandmother's love with a devotion hardly less complete than her own. They lived together in two attic rooms, where they passed the evenings sitting in the dark and talking of their Normandy home. They recalled the past and built endless air castles of the time when they should be able to return. They had grand plans of repurchasing the old cot where both of them had been born, and which had been lost by the foreclosure of a mortgage after the long illness of Pierre's father had ended. They were never tired of talking of what they would do then, and of devising little ways in which the worn-out old farm might be made more profitable. They remained as truly children of the soil as if they had been still in Normandy instead of in their attic in the midst of Paris.

In the daytime Mère Marchette went out to do work as charwoman, while Pierre had been fortunate enough to obtain a place as assistant in a little grocery in Rue M. le Prince. It was in connection with this that Pierre gave his grandmother the only real grief he ever caused her while they were together. Suddenly the boy began to stay away in the evening, and when Mère Marchette sought to know the reason he put her questions aside. One evening as she was making her way home she saw her grandson chatting with a girl at the door of a milliner's dingy shop. The heart of poor old Mère Marchette sunk within her. The castles in the air, from whose glittering towers had shone delusive lights to strengthen and encourage her, fell in ruins before her eyes. In a moment the burden of her age, her poverty, her weariness, seemed increased tenfold. Feebly she climbed the long stairs and sat down to wait, heartbroken. She had all the peasant's instinctive distrust of Paris: she had not been able to live in the Latin Quarter without comprehending something of the evil about her, although, happily for her, the worst features of Parisian life would have been so unintelligible that she might have seen them unmoved. She thought no evil now of Pierre, but she was seized with a terrible fear lest he might fall a victim to one of the sirens of the Latin Quarter, who, to Mère Marchette's thinking, destroyed soul and body alike.

Mère Marchette did not tell Pierre of the discovery she had made. She was only more gentle with him, while in secret she prayed more fervently. For some days longer the lad's mysterious absence continued, the sad hours of the evening stretching like long deserts of agony, over which the soul of Mère Marchette walked painfully with bleeding feet. And then one night Pierre came home with eyes aglow, and all was explained. He put into his grandmother's hand a little pile of francs, a sum pitiful enough in itself but large to them, and told how a milliner in the street beyond had employed him in moving boxes and clearing out the attics of her house, which were to be remodelled into lodgings. This had been his secret, and in his thought of the joyful surprise he was to give his grandmother he had forgotton the pain she might endure by misunderstanding his absence.

It was such trifles as this that were the great events in the life of Mère Marchette and Pierre. There was a tenderness, an unselfishness, an idyllic devotion in their

love which no amount of wealth, or culture,
or rank could have heightened; but in the
lad's veins was the blood of a soldier, that
stirred hot with the currents of a vigorous
youth. Of the army he had dreamed from
his cradle, and strong as was his love for
Mère Marchette the force of destiny was
stronger. It was the old tragedy of youth
and age, of the absorption of maternal love
and the restless impulses of the boy's heart.
Pierre justified his desire to himself with the
excuse that he could earn more money in
the ranks; but his grandmother knew, only
too well, the force of the instinct he had
inherited. She had seen the same struggle
in the life of his father.

When Pierre was eighteen he shouldered
his musket and marched away, leaving poor
old Mère Marchette as much a stranger in
Paris as when she had come to it two years
before to weep and pray alone. It would
hardly be within the power of words to paint
the anguish which lay between Pierre's depart
ure and that hot July noon when Mère Marchette lay dying at the Salpêtrière. Always
in Paris she had been like a wild thing, càged
and bewildered, confused by the life that
swirled about her in the great city, even
when she had been sustained by the presence

of Pierre. When he was gone the gentle old soul began to die of homesickness and heartbreak. For two years she fought death stolidly but persistently, refusing to acknowledge to herself that she was breaking down under the stress of loneliness and sorrow. She came of a race that died hard, and although she was past eighty she looked forward hopefully to the time when Pierre should leave the army and come back to live with her again.

But the struggle for existence in Paris was hard, even when the joy of working for Pierre sustained her; when he was gone it became intolerable. At the end of two years the strength and courage even of the sturdy Norman peasant woman were exhausted; and then a dreadful disease, which had before shown itself in her family, seemed to take advantage of her weakness to spring upon her. She had been a charwoman in the family of Jean Lommel's mother, and so it came about that through the influence of the young doctor she had been admitted to the Salpêtrière when she was already dying from cancer in the stomach.

There was no patient in the ward who was not of better birth than Mère Marchette. She was of all most deficient in education, in knowledge of the world, in the graces of life; and yet of them all it was only the poor old peasant woman who awakened in the minds of the attendants a glow of genuine affection. There are some people who are born to be loved, and when these rare beings remain worthy of it, neither age, nor poverty, nor sickness can destroy their power of awaking affection. The hired nurses touched their lips to her forehead in kisses given furtively, as if they were surprised, and prepared to be ashamed of the emotion which called from them this unwonted display. The doctors spoke to her in tones unprofessionally soft, while Dr Lommel, who had charge of the ward, treated her with an affectionate courtesy scarcely less warm than that he would have shown to his own grandmother. They all knew that Mère Marchette must die, and from counting the time in weeks they had dropped to days, and then to hours. Indeed it seemed only the old woman's will which kept her alive now until Pierre should come. She had borne all her sufferings without a murmur, but she had not been able wholly to repress the cry of her heart. The young soldier's regiment was in Algiers, and there had been difficulties about his furlough.

Had it been any other death-bed in the hospital to which he had been summoned these difficulties would hardly have been surmounted; but in behalf of Mère Marchette the physicians had worked so zealously that all obstacles were removed and Pierre's leave of absence granted. From the moment she had been told that her grandson was on his way she had been perfectly quiet, and, as the doctor said, had devoted her whole being to keeping alive until Pierre should come.

And on this hot July noon the train which was bringing Pierre was drawing nearer to Paris, and Mère Marchette lay so still that she seemed scarcely to breathe, — so still that one might fancy she would not even think, lest in so doing she exhaust some precious grain of strength and so should die without the blessing of that last embrace.

III.

WHOEVER keeps himself informed of the course of modern scientific investigations is likely to be aware that during the last decade especial attention has been given at the Salpêtrière to that strange physical or psychical force known as hypnotism. M. Charcot, chief of the school of the Salpêtrière, has particularly distinguished himself by his researches. Attacked at first by his professional brethren, it has been his good fortune to live to see the scientific value of hypnotism acknowledged, and to be triumphantly readmitted to the Academy of Sciences, which had at first stigmatized his investigations as mere charlatanism. Charles Féré, an assistant physician at the Salpêtrière, with Richer, Bourneville, and nearly a score other distinguished men, have pursued their investigations with great zeal and thoroughness, and have produced a valuable literature devoted to this intricate subject.

It will be easily understood that all the physicians at the Salpêtrière, and especially the younger men, could not fail to be deeply interested in this new and fascinating branch of science. The facts upon which had been founded the theories of mesmerism, animal magnetism, and other shadowy systems were reduced to order and scientifically tested. M. Charcot and his associates worked with much care and thoroughness, and, without being able to solve the mystery of the force with which they dealt, they proved its value as a therapeutic agent. In the cure of nervous diseases, and in dealing with hysterical patients, they obtained remarkable and satisfactory results. They were even able to alleviate suffering by simply assuring the patient, while in a hypnotic sleep, that he would be free from pain on waking.

To the outside observer no feature of this strange power is more remarkable than the influence the hypnotist may exert over his subject after the trance is broken. A hypnotized person may be told to perform any act on awaking, and, when seemingly restored to his normal condition, bears the impress of that command so strongly that he is urged to obey it by an irresistible impulse. It is quite as easy, moreover, to foist upon the patients the most extraordinary delusions. The subject is told that upon awaking a bottle will seem to be a lamp, a blank card a picture, or any other deception which comes into the mind of the hypnotist; and so perfect is the working of this mysterious and terrible law that the delusion is accomplished to its minutest details.

Dr. Lommel, like all his young confrères, had become intensely interested in all these researches, so like a scientific realization of the fairy tales of the Orient. He had even tried some experiments on his own account;

and when the sufferings of Mère Marchette
became pitifully intense he had ventured to
attempt the substitution of hypnotism for
opiates in relieving her distress. The old
woman had not easily yielded to this influence. Susceptibility to hypnotism is more
apt to be found in hysterical or nervously
sensitive subjects than in such sturdy char-
acters. By degrees, however, Dr. Lommel
established control over her. In the end,
to throw her into a hypnotic sleep he had
only to hold his forefinger an inch or two
from her forehead, so that her eyes in
looking at it turned upward and inward a
little. He did not experiment with Mère
Marchette; he felt too tenderly toward the
old woman to make her the subject of scientific investigation outside of the direct line
of treatment. He simply said, " When you
awaken you will be free from pain, Mère
Marchette; " then he would breathe lightly
on her forehead and the sick woman would
awaken, to lie as peaceful and painless as if
no terrible disease was gnawing like a tiger
at her vitals.

The case had attracted a good deal of attention at the Salpêtrière, and although Mère
Marchette was utterly ignorant of it, her sick-
bed was a point of interest toward which

were turned the thoughts of physicians over half of Europe. The unlearned peasant, to whom the simplest terms of science would have been unintelligible, was furnishing data for future scientific treatises; and people of whose very existence she was unaware read the daily bulletins of her condition with closest eagerness.

IV.

It was a few minutes after twelve o'clock when Dr. Lommel reëntered the ward. Mère Marchette lay apparently sleeping, but as he approached her bedside the old eyes opened with a piercing and eager question. The young man shook his head, smiling tenderly.

"Not quite yet, Mère Marchette," he said; "there are still some minutes to wait."

He sat down beside the bed and laid his fingers on her wrist. The pulse was so faint that he could scarcely feel it, but it was steady. For some minutes he remained quiet, with his eyes fixed on the poor old face before him. There came into his mind the thought of what this woman's life had been: her childhood and youth in the hut of a Norman peasant; of what her own home might have been when she became a wife and mother; of the desolation which had come upon her in the death of all her family save only Pierre; of the strange fate that had brought her to Paris; of the terrible wrench which her old heart must have felt when her grandson was taken from her; and of the pathetic patience with which she had borne privation, loneliness, and suffering.

He knew only the outlines of her history, since Mère Marchette had spoken little of herself. What her feelings might have been he could only imagine: the old woman could not have told her mental experiences; she had never even analyzed them. Unless he had been a peasant and a mother himself, Lommel could not have divined Mère Marchette's emotions; he could only reflect what he should have felt in her place. He said to himself at last that, after all, the circumstances which made Mère Marchette's lot so pathetic must also have deadened her sensibilities and so have softened her suffering.

He sighed and looked at his watch. His assistant had gone to the railway station to meet Pierre, and the time he had fixed for their return was already past by five minutes. He felt again of his patient's pulse, with a terrible dread lest after all the young soldier should arrive too late. The artery throbbed more feebly, but still steadily; and at his touch the sick woman opened her eyes with the old questioning look.

" Patience, Mère Marchette," he said, nodding encouragingly; " all goes well."

She did not speak, but she gave him a look so eloquent with gratitude that words were not needed. Then she lay quiet again and the silent watch went on. Five minutes passed, ten, fifteen; the young doctor became extremely uneasy. At last in the distance he heard a clock strike one. At the sound Mère Marchette opened her eyes with a quick, startled glance.

" Pierre ! " she cried, in a voice of intense love and terror.

" Victor has gone to the station to meet him; patience yet a little."

The old woman regarded him with a look of terrible pathos.

" God could not let me die without seeing Pierre," she murmured.

At that moment, through the still afternoon, was heard the sound of a carriage. Mère Marchette's eyes shone with a wild and fevered expression.

" You must be calm," Lommel said. " I will bring him to you."

He administered the little stimulant she could take, and passed quickly out into the corridor.

V.

DR. LOMMEL closed the door of the ward behind him and started down the corridor, but at the first step he stopped suddenly with a terrible sinking of the heart. Victor was coming toward him, but alone, and with a white face.

"Victor," Jean cried, in a voice intense but low, "what has happened? Where is Pierre?"

"There has been an accident," Victor returned. "A bridge broke under his train."

"But you do not know —" began Lommel.

"Yes," the other interrupted; "M. de Brue, who was on the train and escaped with a broken arm, was in the same compartment with Pierre. He rode through on the engine that came in for help. Pierre had told him I was to meet him, and so when M. de Brue saw me he stopped to say that the soldier was struck on the chest and killed instantly."

Dr. Lommel stood regarding his companion with terror and compassion in his look.

"O *mon Dieu!*" he said; "poor Mère Marchette!"

"It will kill her," Victor responded.

"That is nothing," was the doctor's reply. "It is not death, but the agony she will suffer."

At that moment the nurse came out of the ward and hurried down the corridor to join them.

"M. le Docteur," she said, "I beg your pardon, but the excitement of Mère Marchette is so great that I venture to suggest that her grandson hurry."

She glanced around as she spoke, and saw that he was not there. An exclamation rose to her lips; the doctor checked her by a glance.

"Go back to Mère Marchette," said he, "and say that I am cautioning Pierre — Stay, I will go myself. Wait here, Victor."

He went back into the ward and passed down between the cots, from which eyes that the indifference of illness scarcely left human, watched him with faint curiosity. Mère Marchette was sitting up in bed, trembling with eagerness and excitement. All the reserve which she had maintained for weeks had been swept aside. The moment for which she had kept herself alive had come at last, and there was no longer any need to save her energy. Her eyes shone, a feverish glow was on her cheek, even her withered lips had taken on for the moment a wan and ghostly red. It seemed to the doctor, as he looked at her, as if all the vitality which remained in her feeble frame was being expended in a last quick fire.

"Ah," he said, "I have been warning Pierre to be calm, when it is you to whom I should speak. Come, it will take only a moment, but I must give you treatment before I can let you see him."

As he spoke he put his forefinger up to her forehead with a gesture he always used in hypnotizing her. Mère Marchette struggled a moment as if she could not yield to anything which delayed her reunion with Pierre; then she sank into a hypnotic sleep. The doctor leaned forward and spoke with an emphasis which he had never before used with his patient.

"When you awake," he said, " you will see Pierre; the person I shall bring to you is your grandson. Remember," he repeated, " it is Pierre who will come in with me."

He breathed on her eyelids in the usual method of awaking her.

"Now," he said, "I will bring him, Mère Marchette."

He went back to where Victor and the nurse were awaiting him.

"Victor," he said quickly, "you know the experiment M. Charcot tried yesterday when he made a hypnotized patient believe one person was another; I have told Mère Marchette that you are Pierre. You must take his place; come quickly."

The young man drew back.

"I cannot," he protested.

"You must," Lommel returned, almost fiercely. "Come."

VI.

It was with terrible inward misgiving that Jean and Victor entered the ward; but as soon as the eyes of Mére Marchette fell upon the latter they knew that the experiment was a success. Such a look of yearning love illumined the withered old features, such an unspeakable joy shone in the sunken eyes, such quivering eagerness was expressed by the outstretched hands, that the young men found their way to the bedside blinded by tears. An inarticulate cry, that was half moan and half sob, burst from the lips of Mère Marchette as Victor fell on his knees by the bedside. Carried out of himself by genuine feeling, the young man had no need to simulate the emotions necessary for the part he was playing. Seizing the wrinkled hand which lay before him on the bed he covered it with tears and kisses; then, with a cry of piercing sweetness, Mère Marchette flung herself forward into his arms.

"O Pierre, Pierre!" she sobbed. "Oh, the good God, the good God!"

She clasped her arms about his neck, she strained him to her breast, the feebleness of her dying embrace transformed to strength by the divine fervor of maternal love. She mingled her kisses with a soft and hardly articulate babble of endearing words; the terms which she had used over his cradle she mingled with the pet names of his childhood and the loving speech which belonged to maturer years. She held him away from her that she might look at him, and her eyes were holden so that she saw in his face the changes that her fancy had pictured in thinking of the real Pierre.

"Ah," she said, "how brown thou hast grown; and thou art such a man now! Ah, thou rogue," she went on, laughing softly, "I knew thou hadst grown a beard — and not a word of it in thy letters. But I knew."

She put her thin fingers under his chin and with a sudden gravity lifted his face.

"Look in my eyes," she said ; "why dost thou turn away? Hast thou not been a good boy ; hast thou not loved the good God?"

Poor Victor, overwhelmed with the dreadful consciousness of deceit, found it almost impossible, in face of this touching and pious affection, to meet the old woman's glance. He struggled to force himself to look into her eyes unwaveringly. Dr. Lommel laid his hand upon his companion's shoulder.

" Yes, Mère Marchette," said he, " Pierre is a good lad ; that I will answer for."

The old woman raised her eyes toward heaven, and her lips moved. She was evidently praying. She had received extreme unction just before noon, but this moment in which she commended her grandson to God was to her no less solemn than that of her own last communion. Then she put out her hand to Dr. Lommel with her smile of wonderful sweetness and an air of noble simplicity.

" You have been so kind to old Mère Marchette," were her words; "the good God will reward you."

He looked at the old dying peasant woman and tried to speak, but his sobs choked him. He bent and kissed her hand and laid it back gently in that of Victor. Her little strength was evidently failing fast. With a last effort she made a movement to drag herself nearer to Victor. He understood her wish and supported her in his arms.

" Promise me," she murmured, her voice wasted almost to a whisper, " that thou wilt be good."

" I promise," he answered.

And the words were no less sincere because she mistook the speaker. A smile of heavenly rapture came over her face ; she tried to speak and failed. But Victor understood her wish and kissed her. As their lips parted she sighed quiveringly.

" She is dead," said Dr. Lommel.

VII.

VICTOR laid the body gently back upon the bed and rose to his feet. He seized his friend by the shoulders ; the tears were streaming down his cheeks.

" O *mon Dieu,* Jean ! " he cried, " to deceive such trust. I feel as if I had been violating a sacrament."

" I know," the other answered ; " but ah, how happy she was ! "

Interlude Fifth.

"SUCH SWEET SORROW."

"SUCH SWEET SORROW."

Parting is such sweet sorrow.
Romeo and Juliet, ii. 2.

[*A drawing-room. Fanny Motley, who has been making a long call upon her bosom friend, Alice Langley, has at last risen to go.*]

Alice. Oh, don't go yet. I have n't told you half the things I wanted to.

Fanny. Oh, I must go. I've got to go home to dress for Mrs. Fresco's dinner. *Do* you suppose Jack will be there?

A. He told me he was going.

F. Oh, I do *hope* he won't fail. I do *so* want to joke him about his sleigh-ride with Ella. Do you suppose she wore her hat with the orange plumes? It's awfully unbecoming to her. It makes her look just salmon color.

A. She always had perfectly hideous taste. Do you remember that dowdy gown of green plush and mauve tulle she wore to Kate West's german? It was a perfect dream of horror.

F. Yes; did n't she look *per*-fectly hideous? Well (*moving toward the door*), come and see me just as soon as you can.

A. I 'll come in to-morrow before sewing-circle, if I can, to hear about the dinner. Don't be too hard on Jack. You know he 's *aw*-fully thin-skinned.

F. Oh, I won't be hard on him.

A. (*pausing as they reach the door*) Is that the boa you had Christmas?

F. Yes ; is n't it lovely? But I told mamma I knew she got it because she knew I 'd got to have one, and she 'd got to give me something.

A. How mean of you !

F. Oh, she did n't mind. She 's used to it. Be sure and come in to-morrow.

A. Yes, I will. Oh, did I tell you that Tom Jones has invited Sophia Weston to go to the opera Saturday night?

F. You don't mean it. Has he, really?

A. Yes ; Ethel Mott told me this morning.

F. Do you suppose he is in earnest, after all?

A. Oh, there 's no telling about him. Frank says they bet about it at the club.

F. About him and Sophia?

A. Yes ; whether he 'll propose before Lent.

F. How *per*-fectly horrid ! Men are the *worst* creatures. I declare, I think those dreadful clubs ought to be suppressed.

A. So do I. They do say the most outrageous things. I don't see how they can sit and listen to them.

F. I don't, either.

A. And they talk over all the scandals.

F. Yes, it is simply diabolical. How perfectly sweet it is to have a brother who will tell you all about it.

A. Is n't it? It is almost as good as going myself.

F. Will never tells me a single thing (*moving on into the hall*). Well, be sure you come, and come as early as you can. Good-bye. (*Kisses her.*)

A. Good-bye. That boa is just as becoming as it can be.

F. Do you think so? Clara Martin's makes her look as if she had n't any neck at all.

A. Oh, you can wear anything.

F. Thank you, dear. But then you can afford to say so, because you can wear anything yourself. Would you ask Jack about the orange feathers?

A. Oh, he would n't know. Men never know what girls have on, — except Clarence Key, and he 's a perfect man-milliner. Did I tell you what he said to Kate West at the Westons' tea? I 'd have scratched his eyes out.

F. No ; what in the world did he say?

A. You won't repeat it? Because I told Kate I would n't tell. She was so furious she had to tell somebody.

F. I 'll never tell. What was it?

A. You know that tailor-made gown she wears? The one made of gray corduroy? Well, Clarence

Key asked her if she got it so her husband could have it made into riding trousers, after she was done with it.   Did you ever *hear* such impertinence?

F. He did n't really !

A. He really did !

F. Why, Alice !   I should think she 'd have killed him.   I would.

A. So would I.

F. (*putting her hand on the handle of the door*) Well, good-bye.   Give my love to Blanche when you write.

A. Yes, I will.

F. I shall see you to-morrow?

A. Yes.   Good-bye.

[*Fanny opens the door, and a blast of cold wind rushes in.*]

F. Ugh !   How awfully cold it is.   I wish I had taken the carriage.

A. I went over to Ethel Mott's this morning, and I thought I should freeze to *death.*

F. I hope I sha'n't get pneumonia or anything. I want to go to the Claytons' ball.

A. Oh, do tell me ; what are you going to wear?

F. (*returning and closing the door*) There, that is one thing I wanted to ask you about.   I want you to go in white, and I 'll wear that black lace I had made in New York last winter.   I 've never worn it here at all, and that 's the most stylish gown I ever had in my whole life.

A. Would n't that be striking? We could go in together. I 'll have a new white tulle, and wear my pearls. I 'll make Aunt Alicia lend me hers, too.

F. That will be *too* lovely.

A. And you 'll wear diamonds?

F. Oh, no. I wore jet in New York. Not a single thing but black about me; not even my fan-sticks.

A. How *per*-fectly enchanting !

F. Will you do it?

A. Of course I will. I 'll buy the stuff to-morrow.

F. We 'll talk about it when you come to-morrow. (*Opening the door.*) I must go this very moment, or I shall *never* get to Mrs. Fresco's.

A. What are you going to wear to-night?

F. That cardinal I showed you the other day.

A. Is n't that rather gorgeous?

F. Oh, it 's going to be a big dinner, you know ; and there 's lots of black lace on it.

A. It must be awfully becoming.

F. It is. If Jack knows anything, he ought to see a difference between that and orange plumes.

A. Ethel Mott told me — Oh, do come in a moment. I 'm simply freezing to death, and I must tell you this.

F. (*once more coming in and closing the door*) Well, do be quick. I ought to have been home long ago.

A. Oh, you 've lots of time.

F. But it takes so long to do my hair.

A. How are you going to wear it?

F. The same old way. I wish somebody 'd invent some new style, — something real nice and becoming. I asked Uncle Calvin the other night if he had n't seen some pretty styles in China, and I wish you could have *seen* the pictures he brought out !

A. What were they like?

F. Like? They were n't like anything. Why, I just *gasped* over them ! Ships, and butterflies, and all sorts of things ; all made out of hair, right on your own head.

A. Not really?

F. Yes, just as I tell you. I never *saw* anything so frightful.

A. It must have been perfectly ghastly !

F. Well, good-bye. Come early. Oh ! what were you going to tell me?

A. To tell you?

F. Yes, — that Ethel Mott said.

A. Oh, she said that Kate West has been corresponding all winter with that West Point cadet she met at Newport last summer.

F. No !

A. Yes !

F. Why, Alice Langley, do you mean it?

A. Ethel said she knew it.

F. I don't believe it.

A. That's what I said.

F. But she's as good as engaged to George Maynard.

A. I know it.

F. I think it's perfectly awful.

A. So do I.

F. Do you suppose he knows it?

A. Oh, no. He's so gone on Kate, he thinks she'd never look at anybody but him.

F. I never heard anything so perfectly amazing in my life.

A. And sometimes, Ethel says, they write each other two letters a week.

F. Two letters?

A. Two letters.

F. In one week?

A. That's what Ethel says.

F. I wonder she doesn't expect the ground to open and swallow her. I never heard of such deceit. Why, she's going to lead the german with George at the Wentworths' next week.

A. I know it.

F. Well, I've always said Kate West couldn't be trusted out of your sight. (*She turns, and opens the door.*) I do believe that every time I open that door it is colder. I know I shall die before I get home, — or freeze my ears.

A. Think how dreadful it would be to freeze your ears. I knew a girl at boarding-school that froze her ears skating one vacation, and they hung down like rags. We used to tell her they were like a spaniel's, and call her Fido. She'd get *perfectly* furious.

F. I don't wonder.

A. It was awfully good fun to see how she tried to pretend she didn't care ; and then, when she couldn't stand it another minute, she'd catch up the very first thing she could lay her hands on, and throw it.

F. (*descending the steps*) I would if I'd been she. Could she wear ear-rings?

A. Oh, not for the longest time, — as much as a year, any way. When we wanted to be especially pleasant, we told her that frozen ears always came off after a time.

F. How horrid !

A. But it was such fun !

F. Good-bye. Be sure and come to-morrow.

A. Yes.

F. And come early.

A. Yes ; I'll come right after luncheon.

F. Don't you think your gown ought to be made just like my black one?

A. Yes ; that would be more effective.

F. And then we can wear our hair just alike.

A. It's a pity you couldn't have some black flowers.

F. Yes. I don't see why the florists don't get up some. Phew ! It's as cold as Greenland. Do go in. You'll get your death cold.

A. Good-bye. Don't tell what I told you.

F. No ; not to a soul. How did Ethel Mott find out about the letters?

A. She would n't tell.

F. Do you suppose she really knew, or only guessed?

A. She said she really and truly knew.

F. Is n't it amazing?

A. It is *per*-fectly incomprehensible.

E. Well, good-bye. I hope you 'll have good luck at the Whist Club to-night.

A. Oh, do come back till I tell you what Mr. Fremont said about the Whist Club.

[*Fanny returns to the foot of the steps, and Alice goes half way down to meet her.*]

A. He said he was n't going to the Whist Club any more, and I asked him why not, and he said he was tired of taking girls down to feed, when they 'd been talking so all the evening that he could n't play.

F. Why, I never heard anything so insulting !

A. I told Mr. Van Bruch, and he said the trouble was that Mr. Fremont wanted all the time to feed himself.

F. Good. Do you know Colonel Graham says that he went to the Vaughns' to play whist, and they held a conversazione instead. Was n't that clever?

A. Yes ; awfully.

F. Good-bye. I 'll tell Jane to lay out my black dress, so it will be all ready when you come.

A. I 'll try and get time to go down town in the morning, to see what I can get to make my gown of. It 's an awful shame you had to hurry away so ; I had lots of things to say.

F. Well, I really had to go, you know. You can't keep a dinner party waiting, of course.

A. Oh, of course not. Good-bye. I 'm awfully glad you came.

F. Good-bye. I 've had a lovely time.

[*She at last really goes, and Alice, after lingering a second to regret the things she has not said, retires and closes the door of the now pretty well aired house.*]

Tale the Sixth.

———•———

BARUM WEST'S EXTRAVAGANZA.

BARUM WEST threw down his pen, and looked about his attic with a gloomy face. The light from his one window, a dormer facing the east, was too faint to permit his writing any longer, even had he been in the mood; and how far he was from desiring to go on with his work was shown by his seizing the sheets which were the result of his afternoon's labor, and angrily tearing them into bits.

The room was not unlike the traditional abode of that melancholy thing, a poor-devil author. The roof sloped from the middle of the ceiling almost to the floor, the niche of the dormer-window where his writing-table stood being the only part of the eastern side of the chamber where one could stand upright. In the corner on the opposite side stood an old-fashioned, high-posted bedstead; a bureau, over which hung a tarnished mirror of antique frame, was placed opposite the tall stove, in which was carefully cherished a frugal coal fire ; a black trunk was pushed under the eaves, while some pine shelves held the young man's unimposing library. Both carpet and wall-paper were dingy and faded, and in the darkening winter twilight the attic was gloomy enough to depress the spirits of one in a frame of mind far more cheerful than that in which West found himself.

Most authors are too unhappily familiar with the fact that a financial crisis is apt to be so desperately unproductive of marketable ideas that even the excitement of a definite order is likely, at such a time, to beget in the brain rather a confused sense of impotence than a creative inspiration. One must be well seasoned in the vicissitudes of a literary career to be able to do his best under the combined pressure of sore need and the necessity of seizing at once an unusual opportunity. West was still young in his profession, as well as in years, and the wild exhilaration of receiving a conditional commission had given place to an awful feeling of despairing helplessness. A friend who had considerable confidence in him, and, what was more to the purpose, some acquaintance and influence in theatrical circles, had persuaded a manager to promise to consider an extravaganza from the pen of the would-be playwright, and Barum felt as if his whole future depended upon his success.

He had started upon his task with the utmost hope and confidence. He had for a couple of years been studying stage work, writing plays that nobody would touch, and serving that dreary apprenticeship which comes before literary success, but which is, unhappily, not always followed by it. He had pinned above his writing-table a sentence from " Earl's Dene," which had afforded him a sombre support often enough: " The only road to the skies, Mademoiselle, is up the garret stairs. Mozart climbed them, Moretti climbed them, . . . everybody who has ever done anything has had to climb them; and you, Mademoiselle, are one whose duty for the present is to starve." It may have been because he secretly felt that he had starved long· enough, or from the buoyant hope pathetically natural to youth, that West was convinced that his time had come; but at least of that fact he had no doubt.

When, however, he sat down to write, he found his brain teeming, in place of valuable ideas, with the single notion that this time he must succeed; instead of a plot, his mind spun visions of coming greatness; and in place of elaborating witticisms, his thoughts turned alternately to dismal memories and to yet more gloomy forebodings. To-day ended a week of futile endeavor, and the unlucky writer was forced to confess to himself that, so far from being further on in his work than he was seven days earlier, he had stuck where he set out, and acquired the fatal hindrance of a self-distrust which benumbed all his powers.

It grew quickly darker as he brooded, the brief February twilight shutting down rapidly. It was so dark when at last he got heavily upon his feet that he was obliged to fumble about for his shabby hat and coat in the shallow closet which held his scant wardrobe. He muttered to himself as he did so a quotation from Octave Feuillet. He could hardly have been an aspirant for literary honors, and not be crammed to the throat with quotations.

" ' *Ce n'est donc pas un vain mot, la faim !* ' " he said aloud, with so much bitterness that a hearer, had there been one, might have forgiven his sentimentality. " ' *Il y a donc vraiment une maladie de ce nom-là.*' "

He went down the three flights of stairs which lay between his chamber and the sordid street, taking his way to a cheap restaurant, which his soul loathed, but to which the narrowness of his purse constrained him.

The waiter-girls, gossiping together, knew his shabby figure too well to hasten to serve him with any alacrity born of expectation or tips; but one of them came to stand, leaning by one hand upon the table, while he studied the bill of fare in a vain attempt to discover some dish which would be alike satisfactory to his appetite and his finances. There were stains of coffee and of soup upon the card, which gave him a feeling of disgust, as if his food had been served in an unwashed dish; but he repressed his feelings and made out his meagre order. The damsel filled him the usual glass of ice-water, tossed an evening paper before him, and betook herself to cry the supper he had called for into the mouth of a rubber tube, which hung flabbily out of the wall. West could hear the voice of somebody under ground repeating the order, like a surly subterranean echo, and he was peevishly half inclined to fling a plate at the head of a man at the next table, on the supposition that that individual might have been listening to this double disclosure of the straitness of diet to which his poverty constrained him.

He tried to interest himself in the paper which had been given him. He picked out the smallest paragraphs with a feeling of being

so much at variance with the world in general
that nothing could possibly interest him which
was not held to be of no especial moment to
the majority. Suddenly he felt that little thrill
with which a man always comes upon his
name in print. Among a lot of brief jottings
was the statement that a man in Chicago had
left two hundred thousand dollars to Barum
West. For a moment his heart seemed to
stand still, but instantly his common sense
reasserted itself, and he smiled with the bitter
but fleeting cynicism of youth at the impossibility that a fortune should come to him by
any lucky throw of Fortune's dice. The name
was sufficiently uncommon, however, to make
the coincidence striking, and what artistic
youth, so placed that his wits were more or
less disconcerted by the unevenness of life,
could fail to make the paragraph the starting-
point for a thousand dreams.

All that night, when he should have been
sleeping, and when he really was half under the
influence of slumber, Barum West's thoughts,
which should have been devising stage situa-
tions, droll dialogue, and popular allusions,
occupied themselves with that illusive fortune. He considered what he would do did
he really have it; how he would enjoy it;
what delights he would purchase, and what

miseries escape. In dreams his fancy wove
a gorgeous tissue of enchantment, at which
he smiled when he waked, although in reality
it was little more extravagant than the airy
fabric of his waking fancies. When once an
imaginative youth gives rein to his fancy, especially if hope and need prick the tricksy
steed forward, there is no telling to what
lengths the race it runs may not stretch.
West certainly did not believe that the leg-
acy of which he had seen mention was really
intended for his pocket, and yet the coincidence of the name seemed to him so good
proof that it went far toward persuading him
that he was, in truth, the legatee. For the
rest, he, perhaps not unconsciously, humored
a little a dream which at least amused for the
time being a life all too little lightened by
frivolity of any sort.

It was not until the following evening that
it occurred to West that, having a fortune in
hand, it would be necessary for him to invest
it. He was once more at the eating-house,
which to-night he regarded with less bitterness than hitherto, so strong was the effect
of his dream in putting him in better temper
toward life and the world. As he scanned
the paper, in the hope that he might come
upon some further information in regard to

Barum West's fortune, his eye lighted on the stock reports, and, with a sudden sense of importance he reflected that with two hundred thousand dollars to take care of it behooved him to furbish up whatever knowledge he possessed of stocks. The unintelligibility of the stock reports was sufficient proof that he had little knowledge to furbish, but this only aroused his combativeness, and made him determined to learn.

When he left the restaurant he bought a paper of his own, and taking it to his room, he passed the evening in studying finance as represented in the columns of the daily journal. There was something amusing, or pathetic, as one might look at it, about the absorption with which he gave himself to the occupation of deciding what he should do with $200,000 if he had it. He reflected shrewdly that it were wise not to invest his whole capital in a single stock, and he tried to recall whatever he had heard of the relative safety of different classes of security. He guessed at the amount of commission he would be obliged to pay a broker, his guide being a confused remembrance that in a play he had heard a certain rate mentioned. He carefully tabulated his investments, and retired at length, the possessor of an income

of something over $11,000, all commissions
having been paid.

It was perhaps not strange that Barum
was in absolute ignorance of the fact, since
a knowledge of the vagaries of the stock
market was decidedly outside of his world,
but the truth was that he had begun to man-
age his fancied fortunes on a falling market
when the bears were raging in Wall Street.
While he slept that night a combination was
being completed which was the next day to
run down twenty-five per cent the conserva-
tive railroad stock in which West had felt it
safe to put half his fairy gold.   When Barum
took up the paper at the restaurant on the
third evening he had lost about $40,000, — a
fact which could hardly have caused him
more chagrin had he really possessed the
money to lose.

The game he was playing interested him
like a new novel. His quick imagination
had taken fire, and this defeat spurred him
to a fresh endeavor. He felt himself in
honor bound to regain what he had lost;
and this evening went like the last, in com·
plicated and decidedly amateurish efforts to
bring his imaginary finances into a satisfactory condition. The writing of the play of
which he was to read the skeleton to the

manager in a fortnight advanced not at all.
He took his pen to write, and laid it down
to refresh his memory on the latest quotation
on some stock; he tried to think of his plot,
and found himself reflecting concerning de-
benture bonds and second mortgages, with
the vaguest possible notion of what either
might be.

The strange possession which a vivid fancy
may take of a lonely and imaginative mind
is a phenomenon not unfamiliar to those who
have studied the lives of men of fervid temperament; and the whim to which West now
gave himself up was no more extravagant
than many another which has had consequences far more serious.   For days he went
on, becoming more and more completely engrossed by the folly he was following.   His
writing-table was covered with papers upon
which he had memoranda of stocks, of
sales, of investments, calculations of commissions, and all the rest of it.   He even
thought of going down town to watch the
bulletin boards at some broker's, but he
would hardly have been the fanciful dreamer
he was, had he not shrunk from actually
coming in contact with men and the reality
of the business at which he played.

For a week this absurdity continued.   Some-

times West gained a little in his visionary
speculations, and this inspired him with new
courage, although whether he won or lost he
was still possessed with the fatal gambling
mania. His work meanwhile was not advancing. It is true that he sat for hours at
his table nominally at work upon his play,
but he interrupted himself constantly to consider whether there were not some way of recovering the money he had lost.

When Saturday night came he looked back
over his week with regret and shame. The
date fixed for his presenting his sketch to the
manager was now only eight days off, and he
was practically no further advanced in his
preparation than on the day when his friend
brought him the delightful news that that
elusive personage had consented to make
the appointment. He had wasted the past
week in a foolish day-dream, as profitless as
it was absurd. Yet he smiled to himself at
the reflection that his day-dream had at least
been amusing. It had been like creating a
story or the plot for a play; and with a char-
acteristically bachelor thought, he added to
himself that it was at least less dangerous
to play with visions of fortune than of love,
and quite as sensible.

He could not, on the whole, however, be

satisfied with the result of his week, and he
determined to have no more of this folly.
He must set to work in earnest, and he re-
sented the consciousness which forced itself
upon him that his lonely life and imaginative
turn made it possible for him to fall into vagaries which to the practical common-sense of
mankind in general would be held to indicate
anything but a sound mind. He started up
suddenly and gathered all the papers upon
which were recorded his unlucky stock trans-
actions, and began to thrust them into the
stove. He would make an end of the whole
foolish business. And yet, so far from entirely burning his ships, he at least left for
himself a little boat in which to continue his
explorations into the delusive regions of
financial fairy-land, since he saved the one
slip which contained the statement of the
present condition of his much-diminished
fortune. He condescended to the weak, but
eminently human trick of attempting to humbug himself in regard to his reasons for doing
so. He said to himself, exactly as if he were
explaining to another person, that the bit of
paper would serve as a warning to him,
should he ever be tempted to indulge in so
idiotic a diversion again ; and he added, as if
to quiet the least suspicion that he meant to

use the memorandum, that the morrow being Sunday there would be no market with which he could play.

And yet, so weak is human resolution, such a rope of sand is it to fetter the resistless progress of character, — which is destiny, — that the next evening found West with the Sunday paper spread before him, carefully studying the financial article, and elaborating his plans for a grand *coup*, by which he should regain all the thousands he had lost. He had become very canny during the week's study of the market reports, and he felt this Sunday evening all the pleasant satisfaction of one who, out of sight, cunningly devises the overthrow of clever enemies. On Monday morning he would — in imagination, of course — go into the field with a shrewdly devised scheme of buying and selling, which should result in the triumphant re-establishment of his financial standing. When one is dealing with life in imagination merely there is of course no limit to the extent to which one may make himself master of events; and partly from a keen fancy, partly from pure *naïveté,* West's plan involved nothing less than bulling the market himself upon his visionary capital, now shrunken to some $70,000.

All day Monday West was in a state of excitement which was amazingly absurd when one considers that the cause was wholly fancy. When a drunkard returns to his cups he is notoriously more intemperate than before, and in delivering himself up for a second time to the intoxication of his vagaries Barum plunged more recklessly than ever into its extravagances. On Tuesday he was once more to be rich, and then he would speculate no more. Safe mortgages and government bonds should suffice him as investments, even though the rate of interest they paid was low. He would not again expose himself to the chances of such feverish excitement as that in which he had spent the past week.

So real had the whole business become to him that, while he smiled at his own folly as he took up the Tuesday evening paper, he actually felt a pang of disappointment to discover that his imaginary operations had produced no effect on the stock market. So far from rising, stocks had that day gone almost out of sight, so great had been the fall in the price of securities of all sorts.

A feeling almost of despair came over the young man as he read. He had gone out into the street to buy the earliest edition which would contain the account of the sales that day, and as he walked toward his attic he experienced almost as sharp a pang as if the absolute wreck which he found had overtaken his imaginary fortune had befallen a genuine bank-account. That unreasonable youthful disappointment which arises from a sense of failure *per se*, with little reference to the real importance of the stake, stung him keenly; and he was one of those men who cannot but confound real and æsthetic grievances.

He returned to his attic and figured it out. He was absolutely and hopelessly ruined. He had not only lost every dollar of his imaginary fortune, but he was, on paper, some seven or eight hundred dollars in debt to his brokers for commissions. He was so overwhelmed by this catastrophe that he sat brooding over it in the darkness of the February twilight and gathering night, until it was far past the hour when he usually took his apology for a dinner. He was not without a sense of humor sufficiently vivid to make him laugh at himself, and mentally mock at the vexation which the result of his airy speculations caused him; but this did not prevent his being vexed, or take his thoughts from laborious calculations how a different result might have been reached. He went off to dinner at last with a sober

and abstracted mien, ordering a repast even
more economical than usual, as befitted one
who had just lost his whole fortune in ill-
starred speculation.

It was his custom to time his visit to the
restaurant so as to dine before the crowd
of customers came for their evening meal.
To-night, however, he was behind them.
The place was no fuller than he usually
found it, but it bore signs of the recent
crush. The cloth of the table was crumpled
and soiled, the glass in which the inevitable
ice-water was poured was yet warm from
being washed, while the evening paper the
waiter gave him was adorned with an irregular stain of coffee. In the midst of the brown
blotch of this stain was a patch undiscolored;
and by one of those odd and improbable coincidences of which life is full, in the midst
of this spot of dingy white Barum West once
more caught sight of his own name. The
whimsical fate which had started the fantastic
train of thought in his mind ten days before
now finished its work by a paragraph stating
that the will by which $200,000 had been
bequeathed to Barum West by Richard Gran-
ger, of Chicago, was now found to antedate
a second testament by which the money was
left to Harvard College.

Barum West went home with the light step of a boy. A great responsibility seemed suddenly lifted from his shoulders. The capricious fancy which had insisted that he should be depressed because he had lost an imaginary fortune had apparently been willing to accept the fact that even in hypothesis the possession of the money had been a mistake, and the unlucky speculator was formally acquitted at the bar of his inner consciousness. He lit his lamp and his pipe, seated himself in his chintz-covered rocking-chair, with his heels on the top of the coal stove, and ruminated. He reflected upon the fact that it was only five days before he was to meet the manager, and nothing was done in the way of a play which he could for an instant regard as at all satisfactory.

"Instead of writing an extravaganza," he thought, with mingled amusement and self-reproach, "I have been living one."

The form of the thought struck him instantly. His feet came down to the floor with a crash, and in his excitement his pipe went smashing down beside them.

"By Jove!" he cried aloud, "I have it!"

And the plot of the extravaganza, which everybody will remember as being so successful the following winter, "A Speculator in Air," and which set Barum West on his feet financially, was only a properly modified version of the vagaries in which the author had indulged in the handling and the losing of his imaginary fortune.

Interlude Sixth.

———◆———

A BUSINESS MEETING.

A BUSINESS MEETING.

*[Certain absurd, not to say malicious, reports hav-
ing been circulated in regard to the meeting held by
the Rosedale Sewing-Circle to decide upon the time,
place, and other details of their annual spring fair, it
is deemed but simple justice to the estimable ladies who
compose that body to give an accurate and unvarnished
account of the proceedings on that occasion; and the
writer feels that not only will such a narration sufficiently silence all slanders, but that it will as well
go far toward a triumphant refutation of the often-
repeated falsehood that women have no aptitude for
business.]*

THE meeting, being appointed for 2.30 P. M.,
was called to order by the president, Mrs. Gilflora
Smithe, at 3.30 P. M., the hour preceding having
been spent in an animated and pleasant discussion
of the important question whether the pastor's
wife, who was detained at home by illness, was
really so extravagant as to use granulated sugar in
her sweet pickles, as was positively asserted by
Miss Araminta Sharp. The secretary read the
report of the last meeting, as follows : —

" Monday, April 7. — Meeting called to order
by the president. The records read and approved.
There being no quorum present, it was unani-

mously voted to hold the next meeting on Thursday, as that day is more convenient for the ladies. On motion of Mrs. Percy Browne, voted to appoint a committee of one to take charge of the Art Department of the fair. Mrs. Browne kindly volunteered to serve as that committee. Adjourned."

The records having been approved, the president remarked that there was so much business to come before the meeting that she really could not tell where to begin, and she should be glad if some one would make a motion, just to start things.

"A motion to put things in motion," murmured Miss Keene, looking around with the smile which everybody knew meant that she had made a joke.

Everybody smiled also, although nobody saw the point until the president echoed, with a pleased air of discovery, " Motion, — motion ! Very good, Miss Keene."

Then they all smiled once again, and Miss Gray told of an excellent jest made by a cousin in Boston : —

" My cousin in Boston — that is, she is n't my real cousin, but a step-cousin by marriage — was at a concert once, and she made an awfully good joke. I don't remember exactly now what it was, but it was awfully funny. It was something about music, and we all laughed."

" It does n't seem to me," spoke up Miss Sharp, acidly, " that Boston jokes will help the fair much ;

and I move you, Mrs. President, — if I don't make a motion, I'm sure I don't know who ever will, — that the fair be held on the 20th of April."

" I second the motion," promptly spoke up Miss Snob, who always seconded everything.

" It is moved and seconded," said the president, " that the fair be held on the 20th of April; but I'm sure the 23d would suit me a great deal better."

" Why not have it the 17th?" asked Miss Keene; " that seems to me quite late enough."

" Oh, dear, no," interrupted Mrs. Percy Browne, " I never could get half the things done for my department by that time. I move we have it the 30th."

" Second the motion," promptly responded Miss Snob.

" It is moved and seconded," propounded Mrs. Smithe from the chair, " that the fair be held on the 30th. That seems to me an excellent time. If it be your minds, you will please to signify it. It is a vote."

" I still stick to the 20th," declared Miss Sharp, viciously. " I shall open my candy-table then, whether the rest of the fair is ready or not."

" Sweets to the sweet," murmured Miss Keene, looking around with her jest-announcing smile.

" The 20th is Sunday, any way," observed the Hon. Mrs. Sampson Hoyt, in tones of great condescension.

"I don't care," persisted the contumacious Sharp. "I'll have my part of the fair then, any way."

"Suppose we compromise," suggested the president, pacifically, "and say the 25th."

There was considerable discussion, more or less acrimonious, at this proposition, but it was finally adopted without the formality of a vote, the secretary being instructed to set the date April 25th down as the final decision of the meeting.

"There will have to be a general committee of arrangements," the president observed, this important preliminary having been settled. "I suppose it is customary for the chair to appoint them; but I am ready to receive nominations."

"I nominate Miss Keene," said Mrs. Browne, who wished to keep in that lady's good graces.

"Second the motion," Miss Snob exclaimed, with enthusiasm.

"Miss Keene will have enough to do at the cake-table," Mrs. Smithe replied. "I think I'll appoint Mrs. Hoyt, Mrs. Crowler, Mrs. Henderson, and Mrs. Lowell."

"There's never but three on that committee," snapped Miss Sharp. "You'll have to take off one."

"Dear me!" responded Mrs. Smithe, in dismay; "I think you must be mistaken."

But Miss Sharp persisted, and the president, driven into a corner, was forced to propose that one of the ladies named should resign. Nobody seemed willing to do this, however, and it was at length decided that some one of the four should regard herself as a substitute, to act in case one of the others could not serve. The president could not, however, bring herself to specify which should be the substitute, and was greatly relieved when the conversation was turned by Mrs. Henderson's remarking, —

"Speaking of substitutes reminds me. Did you know that you could make mince-pies without meat? My niece from Bangor — "

[*The talk of the next fifteen minutes is omitted, as being irrelevant, relating exclusively to cooking. At the expiration of that time, the business of the occasion was accidentally reintroduced by an allusion on the part of Mrs. Crowler to some delicious chocolate macaroons which she had eaten at a fair in East Machias.*]

"We really must have some more committees," the president said, recovering herself with a start. "Will somebody make a motion?"

"I don't think Friday is a good day for a fair, any way," Mrs. Lowell now remarked, reflectively. "The 25th is Friday."

"Oh, I never thought of that," exclaimed half a dozen ladies, in dismay. "We should be all tired out for baking-day."

"I don't know what we can do," the president said, in despairing accents, — "there seem to be so many days, and only one fair; and we've had

so many dates proposed.   We shall have to unvote
something."

It was at this crisis that the Hon. Mrs. Sampson
Hoyt rose to the heights of the parliamentary
opportunity.

"I move the previous question," she said, distinctly and firmly.

There fell a hush of awe over the sewing-circle,
and even Miss Snob was a moment in bringing out
her second.

"I don't think!" Mrs. President Smithe ventured, a little falteringly, "that I quite understood
the motion."

"I moved," the Hon. Mrs. Hoyt replied, with
the air of one conscious that her husband had
once been almost nominated to the State Legisla-
ture, and had been addressed as Honorable ever
after, "I moved the previous question."

"Yes?" Mrs. Smithe said, inquiringly and
pleadingly.

"That takes everything back to the beginning,"
Mrs. Hoyt condescended to explain, "and we can
then change the date of our fair in a strictly legal
way."

She threw a glance of superb scorn around her
as she spoke, and even Miss Sharp took on a
subdued and corrected air.

"It is moved and seconded the previous question," Mrs. Smithe propounded, with an air of
great relief.   "It is a vote."

"I don't think we had better do away with everything in this case," Mrs. Hoyt observed, with a smile of gracious concession. "We might let the committee of arrangements stand."

"That she's chairman of," whispered Mrs. Crowler, spitefully.

"I don't remember," observed Miss Sharp, gazing into futurity with an air of abstraction, "that there is anything in the by-laws about the previous question."

A flutter stirred the entire company. The ladies looked at each other, and then with one accord turned their regards upon the Hon. Mrs. Hoyt, as one who, having got them into this difficulty, was in honor bound to help them out of it.

"I supposed everybody knew," that lady remarked, with icy sweetness, "that the rules of making motions do not have to be in the by-laws. They are in"—the speaker hesitated, not being exactly sure of the title of the volume to which her husband had given so careful attention when expecting to be nominated: feeling, however, that anything was better than the appearance of ignorance, she went on precipitately—"in 'Pole's Manual.'"

Even Miss Sharp had no retort adequate to meet this crushing appeal to authority, not being sufficiently well informed to connect Pole with whist, so she contented herself by observing, with a sniff, that for her part she was glad she did not know so much as some people pretended to.

"It does seem to me," observed Mrs. Henderson, at this point, "that we might let this one year go by without a fair. There's been so much sickness in Rosedale this winter that everybody is tired out, and we had a great deal better wait till June, and have a strawberry-festival. I move we put the whole thing off till then."

"Second the motion," cried Miss Snob, with great promptitude.

"I cannot consent to put that motion," the president said, with great dignity. "We have made up our minds to have a fair now, and we might as well have it, and be done with it."

"I move," Mrs. Browne put in sweetly, with the intention of suiting everybody, "that we have a fair *and* a strawberry-festival."

Miss Snob seconded this motion with her customary enthusiasm.

"It is moved and seconded," the president said, "that we have a fair and a strawberry-festival. But that seems a great deal; and I think I had better declare it not a vote, unless doubted."

Nobody was clear about the effects of doubting a negative proposition; but Mrs. Crowler was pleased to observe, "Well, any way, now I come to think it over, I think, on the whole, I won't be on the arrangements committee at all; but I'll be chairman of the finance committee when that is fixed, — and that 'll leave only three on the arrangements."

This moved Mrs. Henderson to resign, and Mrs. Lowell following her example, Mrs. Hoyt was left in solitary grandeur upon the committee.

Matters were not improved, moreover, when Miss Keene remarked, " If we 've voted ' the previous question,' I don't see but we 've still got to fix the day. All that is undone now."

" Certainly," responded the Hon. Mrs. Sampson Hoyt, with the virtuous joy of an iconoclast gazing on the ruin he has wrought.

" We don't seem to have anything exactly fixed," the president said, with a helpless and conciliatory smile. " If somebody would make a motion — "

" It 's too late to make any more motions to-day," Miss Sharp interrupted, with much vigor. " It 's ten minutes of six."

At this announcement of the lateness of the hour, the entire company started to their feet in dismay ; and although, when the president and secretary tried next day to remember what had been done, that the latter might make up her report, they recorded that the meeting adjourned, that statement must be regarded as having been purely a parliamentary fiction, entered in the secretary's book to gratify that instinct innate in woman's breast to follow exactly the regular and strictest forms of recognized rules of order.

Cale the Seventh.

———◆———

A SKETCH IN UMBER.

EVERY life has its history: this is the story of Ruth Welch, the placid-faced, silver-haired woman who sat in the September twilight looking out over the moorlands one Saturday evening, and considering many things.

The house faced toward the south. It looked across a little creek which made in from the sea, and it had in its prospect only level heaths to the horizon's edge. On the west stretched the waters of an arm of the Atlantic, and the tides came twice a day around the low cape into the inlet, and the wind blew over the moors; but in all directions one looked upon level wastes, — "the plains," the country people called them, speaking of them sometimes as "Welch's bogs," or in sections as the "blueb'ry plains," or the "cramb'ry marshes;" and people who lived outside of them regarded the moors as painfully dull.

They were not, too, without some excuse for such an opinion. The rhodora and the

kalmia — the "lamb-kill" — in spring spread
over sections of the waste transient sheets of
glowing color, but for the most part the
country was either white or brown, and to
one not fond of it the effect of the monotone
of hue was depressing. The shade of brown
varied, changing from a grayish or even
greenish brown in midsummer to a sombre,
almost uniform umber in autumn, which latter tint now and then during the winter appeared in desolate patches through the flats of
snow, until in March the whole plain came to
light darker and more forbidding than ever.

All these long months the only break in
the low monochrome of the landscape was
the red cottage which still was called "Gran'-
sir' Welch's," although the old man had been
dead many a year, and the little garden before it that kept up, with old-fashioned flowers, a show of bravery until the frosts came.
The tint of the old house was dull and dingy,
but in so colorless a setting the hue seemed
brighter, as a single event might assume un-
due importance in a monotonous life. If one
could have supposed the builder an imaginative man or one given to refinements of sentiment, it might be easy to imagine that when
he built his house thus alone in the plains,
with not another dwelling in sight and with-

out a break in the level landscape, he felt the
need of giving it some color that should protest against the deadly grayness of all around
and hearten its owner by its warmth of tone.

So overwhelming were the solitude and the
unbroken sameness of the place, however,
that an imaginative man would scarcely have
chosen it as an abiding-place, although once
involved in its powerful fascination he would
have been held to his life's end. By what
accident Gran'sir' Welch's grandfather had
chosen to build here, half a score of miles
from the little fishing village which stood to
the people of that region for the world, no
one knew, and very likely no one cared.
Folk thereabout concerned themselves little
with reasons for anything, facts being all they
found mental grasp sufficient to hold. Once
established in the plains, however, there was
no especial cause to suppose the family would
not continue to live on there until its course
was interrupted either by extinction or by
the arrival of the Judgment-Day.

Extinction was not very far off now, since
only this white-haired woman remained to
bear the name. Her mother had died in the
daughter's infancy. Mrs. Welch had never
adapted herself to the silence and loneliness
of the moors, and her people over at the

village declared that she had " died of the
plains ; " and it is possible that they were
right. Ruth's father, when she was still but
a child, had been lost at sea; and the girl
had been cared for by her grandfather and
the old serving-woman Bethiah, who had once
been supposed to be a hired girl, but had
ended by being so thoroughly identified with
the family that her surname was wellnigh
forgotten, and she was designated, when she
was spoken of at all, as Bethiah Welch.

The child grew much in the same way as
grew the houseleeks in the boxes beside the
southern door, very slowly and dully. Once
or twice she went for a few months to stay
with an aunt in the village ten miles away, it
being the unanimous opinion of her relatives
that as the Welches always had known how
to read and write it was proper that something should be done for Ruth's education ;
and the village school was the only educa-
tional means known in the region. The girl
pined for home, however, and was never content away from the red house. Perhaps by a
strange perversity of circumstance the home-
longing of the mother was in the child transformed into a clinging fondness for the place
where the former was so lonely and alien.
The low, level moors were necessary to

Ruth's life; in their colorless monotony she somehow found the complement for her uneventful life. Perhaps the very dulness developed her imagination, as special organs appear in animals whose abnormal conditions of existence render them needful. If this were so, it was no less true that the moors absorbed whatever mental life they stimulated, until the girl seemed hardly less a part of them than the knolls of leathery shrubs, the scattered, shallow pools, the tufts of coarse grass, or the whispering voices of the wind which all night long and every night were hurrying to and fro, concerned with unspeakable tidings which perhaps came from the sea that forever moaned along the moorland's edges.

Little conscious imagination had Ruth at nineteen; and it was at nineteen that the single, trifling event of her life occurred. She was a maiden by no means uncomely. She was not educated in any conventional sense of the term; but her life alone with her grandfather and old Bethiah and the great brown moors had bred in her a certain sweet gravity which was not without its charm, had there been but those to see who could appreciate it.

Along the front of the house ran a bench, where people seldom sat, since there were

none to sit, but where the milk-pans dried in
the sun, a gleaming row; and one sunny morning late in September the flash of their shim-
mer caught the eye of a skipper who in his
yacht in the bay studied the horizon with his
glass.   He was not yet past those years when
a man still finds amusement in imitating fate
and nature by yielding to his impulses; the
gleam suggested pleasant draughts of fresh
milk; and without more ado, he headed the
trig little craft in which he and a brother
artist were skirting the coast of the Gulf of
Maine for the little inlet upon which Gran'sir
Welch's red cottage stood.

In those days yachts were less common
than now, and both Ruth and Bethiah left
their work to watch the boat as it ran up to
the low wharf, and the snowy sail fell with a
musical rattle and clash of metallic rings.

The skipper, a stalwart young fellow, too
handsome by half, came briskly ashore and
did his errand, and while the old servant
went for the milk, stood with Ruth by the
open door asking idle questions, to which she
replied without either shyness or boldness.
His eyes were just on a level with hers as she
stood on the threshold above him, and their
bold, merry glance saw with full appreciation
how clear were her sherry-brown orbs.   He

removed his cap and leaned against the
door-post, letting his glance stray over the
landscape. Here and there upon the brown
surface his keen eye detected the flame of a
scarlet leaf amid the prevailing russet, but the
combined effect of all the red leaves upon
the plain could not warm the sombre wastes.

"Don't you get tired of the sameness?"
he asked suddenly, as if the monotony all at
once seemed to him too great to be borne.

"Oh, no," Ruth answered, smiling faintly,
"I like it."

He brushed back his curly, golden locks
with a shapely brown hand, and regarded her
more closely.

"It is like a fish in the water," was his
conclusion when he spoke again. "It would
drown me."

Ruth smiled again, showing her white, even
teeth a little, although she did not in the
least understand what he meant; and before
the conversation could go further Bethiah
appeared with the milk she had been getting.
Ruth put aside the stranger's offer of pay,
and with an instinct of hospitality which must
have been genuine indeed to have survived
so long disuse from lack of opportunity, she
stepped down into the little garden-plot and
picked a nosegay of the old-fashioned flowers

which in the southern exposure were still
unharmed by frost.

" Put a posy in my button-hole," he re-
quested lightly, when she gave them to him.
" Pick out the prettiest."

She had never stuck a flower in a man's
coat, but she was too utterly devoid of self-
consciousness to be shy. She selected a
beautiful clove pink, and smiling her grave
smile, thrust the stem through the button-
hole of his yachting-jacket as he held out
the lapel.

"It would be just the color of your cheeks,"
he said, " if it could only get sunburned."

A redder glow flushed up at his words,
and so tempting was the innocent face before him that half involuntarily he bent forward to kiss the smooth lips. The girl drew
back, in that grave, unemotional fashion of
hers which was to the stranger so unaccount-
able at once and so fascinating, and he failed
of his intent.

"Ah, well," he said, in nowise disconcerted,
" keep the kiss for your sweetheart, but thank
you for the flowers."

He laughed with a gleeful, deep-toned note,
and turned down the faintly-defined path to
the shore again.

Ruth looked on with interest at the hoisting of the sail; she smiled responsively as the two mariners doffed their caps to her, and then, regardless of the old superstition of the ill-luck of watching people out of sight, she kept her eyes fixed upon the pretty little craft as it skimmed over the waters, as long as it could be seen. Then she turned a comprehensive glance over all her moors, as if to to take them into confidence regarding the pleasant incident which had just happened, and returned to her interrupted domestic duties. The interview had touched her with no repinings; and even could she have known that in that brief moment all the romance of her life had been acted, she would scarcely have sighed. She smiled as she went about her homely occupations, and flushed a little with the consciousness of innocent vanity as she found herself glancing into the glass at the reflection of her softly-glowing cheeks, reddened with health and with the sun.

This September day was the single glowing spot in the slow, mellow years of Ruth's life. She came and went, slept and waked, perhaps even dreamed. She was always in a happy, contented repose among her moors, becoming of them every day more and more completely a part. The wide plains grew green in spring with transient verdure, the purple petals of the rhodora flushed through their brief day and dropped into the shallow brown pools left by the late rains in the hollows; then all the waste turned to fawn and russet under the suns of summer, and the cycle of the year was completed by deepening browns and the wide stretches of snow. Now and again great rolling masses of mist came up from the sea and hid wold and wave alike from sight, but yet the sense of the plains was like a presence to Ruth, as with heart warm as an egg beneath the motherbird's breast, she went her way and lived her span of life.

She was far from being dull in her feelings. Indeed, for one in her station and surroundings, she was unusually sensitive to mood of shore and sky, to the beauty of the sunsets or of the wild flowers which sprang amid the low shrubs. She was simply content. She was so perfectly in harmony with her world that she could not be unhappy. She grew as a bluebell grows. She was not deficient in womanly sentiment. She thought sometimes of the handsome sailor lad whose bold brown eyes had looked into hers, and she smiled anew with simple pleasure that he had found her fair. She remembered the audacious gleam which crossed his face when

he bent forward to kiss her, and she did not
forget his words about a sweetheart. She
never spoke of her memories, — she came of
a reticent race, and neither Gran'sir' Welch
nor Bethiah was especially adapted to the
reception of confidences, — but she specu-
lated concerning the sweetheart she never
had, and of whose coming fate gave no sign.
There was never any tinge of melancholy in
these reflections. She accepted life too
simply to be sad, even with that vague op-
pression which seemed to casual observers
the obvious consequence of the overpowering
presence of the wastes.

As years went on, she accepted the fact that
the time of dreams of love was past, and with
placid content she reflected that the shadow
of the ungiven kiss of the sailor would never
be disturbed by the pressure of lover's lips
upon hers.

It is between twenty and thirty that the
temperament of a woman becomes fixed, and
all her future irrevocably made or marred.
Before this her character is too flexible, after
this too rigid for impressions to be lasting.
During these years the peace of the wide,
calm, and sombre moorlands stamped indeli-
bly upon Ruth a sweet, grave content which
nothing could destroy or shake.

There came a time when into the calm of
the old house death rushed, with that dreadful
precipitancy which always marks his coming,
even when expected, and old Gran'sir' Welch,
long past fourscore, was, in the quaint language of the King James version, gathered to
his fathers.

In the gray dawn Ruth tapped softly at the
hives of the bees which stood, straw-thatched,
against the eastern end of the cottage, and
announced the sad news, firmly believing
that unless within twelve hours the swarms
were told of death they would desert their
homes. Then in the sunny autumn afternoon a funeral procession of boats trailed
from the red cottage to the graveyard behind
the church in the village, where slept such of
his forefathers as the sea had spared to die in
their beds. With evenly dipping oars went
first the quaintly-shaped pinky bearing the
coffin between two stout fisherman, one at
prow and one at stern; while after followed
the dories in which were the few nearer relatives who had come to attend the services
at the house.

Ruth sat beside a cousin and listened half
unconsciously to the plash of the oars and
the rhythmic beat of the waves against the
boat, looking back with tear-dimmed eyes to

the red house until it was by distance blended with the dun country as the last spark dies amid the ashes. She was sad, and she felt that oppressive terror which the presence of death brings; yet her calm was not seriously or permanently shaken.

In their relentless, even course the years moved on, and one day in spring, when the rhodora was in all its glory, and the one bush of mountain-laurel in the wide plains, which had strayed into the heath like a lamb into the wilderness, was as white in the distance as a bunch of upland maybloom, again Ruth went softly and gravely to tell the bees that death had been in the red house, and the procession of boats, like the Egyptian train over the Lake of the Dead, bore away the mortal remains of faithful old Bethiah.

Ruth's relatives in the village tried to induce her now to come to them, and when she could not be moved to do this, urged her at least to have some one live with her. She was getting to be an old woman, they said among themselves, although in truth she was little past fifty, and since for that part of the world she was not ill-provided with worldly goods, there was no lack of those who were willing to take up their abode as her companion in the red house.

Ruth put all offers aside, — kindly, indeed,
but decisively. She was pleased to live
alone; not from a misanthropic dislike of
her kind, but because it was so deep and
inexhaustible a delight to her to brood happily among her plains. More and more she
loved these umber wastes, over which cloud-
shadows drifted like the darkening ripple of
the wind on the sea. She knew all their
ways, those mysterious paths which wind
between the hillocks of deserted heaths as if
worn with the constant passing of invisible
feet, and she was never weary of wandering
among the ragged hummocks, breathing in
the salt air from the sea and noting with
happy· eyes all the weeds and wild flowers,
the shrubs that were too inconspicuous to be
singled out at a distance, but which to the
careful and loving observer revealed themselves as full of beauty. She was fond of
the faint, sweet scents of the opening flowers
in spring, of the dying grass in fall, of the
burning peat when fires broke out sometimes
to smoulder until the next rain. She never
thought about her feelings or phrased the
matter to herself, but she loved so perfectly
these wastes which seemed so desolate that
they were to her as kindred and home; perhaps even the maternal instinct which is in-

born in every woman's breast found some not quite inadequate expression in her almost passionate fondness for the great heath.

Her relatives spoke of her always as " odd," and were aggrieved that her ways should be different from theirs; but everything that continues comes in time to be accepted, and as the years went on Ruth's method of life came to seem proper because it had so long been the same. A brawny armed fisher cousin sailed over from the village every Sunday morning to see that all was well at the red house, and to bring whatever might be needed from the village store. Sometimes in winter he found her house half buried in snow, but he never could report that she appeared either discontented or sad.

It was of the coming of this emissary that Ruth was thinking on this Saturday night in September where first this record found her. She had been reflecting much to-day about dying. In her walk about the heath she had come upon a dead bird, and the sight had suggested to her her own end. She acknowledged to herself that she was old, and for perhaps the only time in her life her thought had formulated a general truth. She had regarded the tiny corpse at her feet, and then, looking about upon the moors, it

came over her how immortal is the youth of
the world and how brief is man's life. The
land about her was no older than when she
had looked upon it with baby eyes. For a
single instant a poignant taste of bitterness
seemed set to her lips; then in a moment the
very wide, changeless plain that had caused'
her pain seemed itself somehow to assuage it.

To-night sitting here she admitted to herself that her strength had failed somewhat
of late. Yes, she was old. It was almost
half a century ago that that bold-eyed handsome stranger had compared the color in
her cheeks to a clove pink. She smiled
serenely, although her reflections were of
age and death, so perfectly did she recall
the sunny day and the air with which the
sailor would have kissed her. Placid and
content in the gathering dusk, she smiled
her own grave, sweet smile, which it were
scarcely too fanciful to liken to the odor of
the clove pink of her garden-plot whose hue
half a century ago had been in her cheek.
She had but one regret in leaving life, and
that was to leave her moorlands. She had
found existence so pleasant and had been so
well content that she could not understand
why people so usually spoke of life as sad;
but she could not think without pain of

leaving the plains behind and going away to lie in the bleak hillside graveyard where slept her kinsfolk. It had never occurred to her before to consider to which she held more strongly, her people or the wide, brown stretches of open about her, but to-night she debated it with herself and decided it. She resolved to say to her cousin to-morrow that she wished her grave made in the plains. Very likely her relatives would object. They had always thought her ideas strange; but they would surely let her have her way in this. She would even make some concessions and perhaps let Cousin Sarah come to live with her if they would agree to do as she wished about this. It would be so great a comfort to her to be assured that she was not in death to be separated from her dearly loved moors. She liked Sarah well enough, only that it was so pleasant to live alone with her bees and the plains. Besides, if she should chance to die alone, who would tell the bees? It would be a pity to have the fine swarms lost.

Suddenly she started up in the dusk, and without knowing clearly why she did it, she wrote on the bottom of the list of errands which she always made on Saturday for her cousin her wish concerning her grave. The

spot she mentioned was a knoll near the
house, where the ground rose a little before
it dipped into the sea. She reflected as
she wrote that it was wiser to be prepared
for whatever could happen, and, although
she would not own it frankly even in these
lonely musings, Ruth had felt strangely
weak and worn to-day.

She frugally blew out the candle when her
writing was done, and with calm content sat
down again in her rocking-chair by the window darkening to "a glimmering square." She
heard the sound of the sea and the low wind
blowing over the wide plains; and, lulled by
the soft sounds, she fell at last asleep.

The wind rose in the night, and it was
afternoon when the cousin from the village
came in sight of the red house. No smoke
rose from its chimney, and as he tied his
clumsy sail-boat to the low wharf where so
long ago a yacht had been briefly fastened,
a long wavering line of bees rose glistening
from the straw-thatched hives, floating upward and away like the departing soul of
mortal. Their mistress had been dead more
than twelve hours and they had not been
told. Perhaps it was a chance flight; perhaps
they were seeking her serene spirit over the
moors she loved so well.

Interlude Seventh.

THIRTEEN.

THIRTEEN.

[*The drawing-room of Mr. Sylvanus Potts Thompson, banker. Mr. Thompson and his wife, with ten guests, making a neat round dozen in all, are waiting the announcement of dinner. Enter Mr. Sylvanus Potts, a wealthy uncle from the country.*]

Mr. Potts. I told the man there was no need to announce me; you knew I was coming next week, and a few days don't matter. How do you do, nephew? how do you do, Jane?

Mr. Thompson. Why, uncle, we did not expect you so soon, but we are always glad to see you, of course.

Mrs. Thompson. Yes, always, dear Uncle Sylvanus. How is everybody at home?

Mr. P. Oh, they 're all well; you seem to be having a party, nephew?

Mr. T. Only a few friends to dinner. Let me introduce you.

[*He takes him on his arm and presents him to his guests. While this is being done, a sentimental, elderly young woman, with thin curls, after whispering impressively with her neighbor, glides up to the hostess, and holds a moment's conversation with that lady. Mrs. Thompson turns pale, and seems engaged in a mental calculation. Then she starts quickly toward her husband and draws him aside*]

Mrs. T. Sylvanus, do you know how many people there are in this room?

Mr. T. Oh, about a dozen, I suppose.

Mrs. T. About a dozen! There are thirteen, Sylvanus, thirteen!

Mr. T. Well, what of it?

Mrs. T. What of it! Why, we can't sit down to dinner with thirteen at table. Maria Smith says she should have a fit.

Mr. T. But she would n't, my dear; she's too fond of her dinner.

Mrs. T. Mr. Thompson, is it kind to speak so of my most particular friend?

Mr. T. But what does Maria expect us to do about it? Turn Uncle Sylvanus out of the house? Was n't I named for him, and have n't I always been his favorite? Do you want me to be left out of his will?

Mrs. T. But something must be done. Don't you see everybody is whispering and counting? Can't we get somebody else?

Servant (who has entered unperceived). There is a man downstairs, sir, wants you to sign something.

Mr. T. Ah, my dear, here's the very man, — young Jones. He's our new cashier, and a very clever fellow.

[*Exit Mr. Thompson. During his absence Mrs. Thompson communicates to Miss Smith the solution of the difficulty at which they have arrived. Every-*

*body has soon heard of it, so that on Mr. Thompson's
return with Mr. Jones, the pair are greeted with much
joking about the ill-luck which is thus averted. The
necessary introductions take place.*]

Mr. Jones. I am sure I am rejoiced at being
instrumental in bringing good luck.

Miss Smith. You can certainly see how welcome
you are, Mr. Jones.

Mr. J. But I fear it is not for myself, Miss
Smith.

Miss S. That will undoubtedly come later, when
we know you better.

Mr. P. I am glad you found somebody, nephew;
for I must say I never would have given up my dinner for a foolish superstition; and as I came last
and uninvited —

Mrs. T. (*relieved of her fears and remembering
the will*) You are always invited to this house,
Uncle Potts; and we would never hear of your
going away.

Mr. Robinson. Well, it is all very well to call it
a superstition, you know; but I knew —

[*Mr. Robinson proceeds to narrate a grewsome and
melancholy tale, in which disaster and death resulted
from the imprudence of sitting down with thirteen at
table; half a dozen other guests begin simultaneously
the relation of six more equally or even more grewsome and melancholy tales upon the same subject, when
they are interrupted by the arrival of a note for Mr.
Robinson.*]

Mr. R. My dear Mrs. Thompson, I am so sorry,

but my brother has telegraphed for me to come to him at once on a matter of the utmost importance. I regret —

Mrs. T. But Mr. Robinson, don't you see that —

Servant. Dinner is served.

Mr. T. May I have the honor, Mrs. Brown?

Miss S. But we can't go to dinner now. Mr. Robinson is called away, and that leaves us thirteen again.

[*An awful hush ensues, during which Mr. Robinson, finding himself regarded as a criminal, suddenly slips away, leaving the company to extricate themselves from their trying situation as best they can. The hush is followed by a Babel of voices, in which all sorts of suggestions are made.*]

Mr. J. (*with heroic and renunciatory self-denial*) Let me speak, please, Mrs. Thompson. It was very kind in your husband to invite me to remain to dinner, but now that I shall be the thirteenth, I am sure you'll excuse me.

Mr. T. But it seems so inhospitable.

Mrs. T. But it is more generous to deprive ourselves of Mr. Jones's company than to be the means of bringing ill-luck upon him.

Mr. J. Quite right. I bid you good evening, Mrs. Thompson. I sincerely hope nothing further will occur to mar the pleasure of your evening.

[*Mr. Jones having retired, a move is at once made toward the dining-room, but just as Mr. Thompson and Mrs. Brown reach the drawing-room door, they*]

are confronted by Mr. Robinson, who comes in breath-
less but triumphant.]

Mr. R. I thought it was so unkind of me to
throw all your arrangements into confusion after
the ill-luck of numbers you have already had, that
I concluded to telegraph to my brother instead of
going. Phew! How I have hurried! I am glad
I am in time.

Mrs. Brown. Mr. Thompson, I positively cannot
sit down at table with thirteen. My aunt died of
it, and my second cousin. I am positive it runs
in the family, and I know I should be the one to
bear the consequence if we had thirteen at any
table where I sat down.

[*The greatest confusion follows. Miss Maria
Smith is heard to declare that* "Fate takes delight
in persecuting her!" *while young Algernon White
mumbles something which has a distinct flavor of the
Apostles' Creed. Mr. Robinson shows a disposition
to consider himself a most ill-used individual, thus
to be rewarded for the trouble he has taken.*]

Mr. T. My dear, what shall we do now?

Mrs. T. There is only one thing that I can
think of; we can send across the street for Widow
Ellis. You might go yourself and explain to her
how it is.

[*This suggestion being acted upon, the company
settles into a solemn gloom, pending the return of the
host with Widow Ellis. Every one knows the dinner
will be spoiled, none being more acutely conscious of
that fact than the hostess, and every one is nearly per-*

*ishing with hunger. More grewsome and melancholy
stories are told, but in a wavering and subdued manner, as if they are being offered as excuses for resisting
the cravings of appetite, which are rapidly becoming
insupportable. Young White is heard to mutter, with
fresh suspicions of theological terms, that one might as
well die of thirteen at table as of starvation, and that
for his part he prefers the former method of extinction.
The return of Mr. Thompson with the Widow Ellis
awakens some feeble enthusiasm, but it is evident that
nothing short of a substantial dinner can restore the
spirits of the company.]*

Mr. P. Well, nephew, now I hope we may
have some dinner. I, for one, am faint with
hunger.

Mr. T. Oh, immediately. Mrs. Brown, we —

*[At this juncture poor Mrs. Thompson, overcome
with anxiety, fatigue, and hunger, produces a diversion by falling in a dead faint. The shrieks of Miss
Maria Smith are re-enforced by those of other ladies of
the company, and it is to be feared that Mr. Algernon
White no longer enjoys the exclusive privilege of in-
dulging in ecclesiastical references. The excitement
usual upon such occasions reigns, and when at length
Mrs. ·Thompson is restored to consciousness, but is
found to be too ill to stand, and is borne off to her
chamber, the company, once more reduced to thirteen,
distributes itself in a stricken and overwhelmed state
about the drawing-room, with the air of having ceased
to struggle against an adverse fate.]*

Widow E. We are thirteen again, neighbor;
and if you 'll excuse me —

Mr. P. Thirteen or no thirteen, nephew, I'm going to have something to eat if it's in this house.

[*He disappears toward the dining-room, and as the resolution of Widow Ellis seems to have solved once more the dreadful conundrum of the fated number, the company hastily follow, too nearly famished to notice that the lady does not carry out her apparent intention of returning home, so that after all they sit down thirteen at table.*]

Tale the Eighth.

———◆———

APRIL'S LADY.

APRIL'S LADY.

IT was fortunate that when the editor of the "Dark Red" magazine first did me the honor to request a story from my pen, I had one ready for him, and one, moreover, with which I was so well satisfied. I had so long vainly desired to be really asked for a contribution, and thus raised from the numerous and indiscriminate company of scribblers who send hopeful manuscripts to the magazines, and in trembling uncertainty await the issue, that it is not strange my bosom swelled with gratified pride, and that I dispatched my copy with so perfect a sense of complacency that I almost seemed to condescend a little in letting the editor have it.

I was fond of that story. I experienced a certain delight in recalling the circumstances under which it was composed, and I felt in it that confidence which an author is sure to have in work which has sprung spontaneously, and as it were full-grown, from his

brain. Every literary worker, down to the
veriest penny-a-liner of them all, knows the
difference between a tale which makes itself,
so to speak, growing unforced into beauty
and completeness like a crystal, and a laboriously constructed piece of work, be it con-
trived never so ingeniously and cleverly. The
fiction I sent to the editor of the " Dark Red "
was of the former variety. It had come into
my head all of itself, as the children say,
while I was travelling between New York and
Boston, so complete and so distinct that I
scarcely seemed to have more to do with its
creation than the later putting upon paper.

The circumstances were these : —

I had reached the Grand Central Station
just in time to catch the morning train ; and
as the cars swept out into the daylight, I
settled myself into a seat with a comfortable and something too self-satisfied feeling.
In the first place, I was glad to be out of
New York, — partly because it was hot and
dusty there, partly because I am not over-
fond of Gotham, and partly because sundry
pleasant bachelor friends and divers good
times were awaiting me at the Boston end
of the journey.

I looked out upon the sunny landscape,
over which the splendors of an April day

cast a glow of warmth and brightness, smiled
at the remembrance of a retort I had made
at the Century Club on the previous evening,
which seemed to me rather neat, and then
with a sort of mental nod of farewell to all
the outside world I took up my book and
prepared to follow the fortunes of the woful
and wicked, but thoroughly charming French
heroine with whose adventures I was at that
particular time occupying myself.   To my
vexation, however, I discovered that instead
of the second volume I had taken the first,
and as I had no especial desire to peruse
again the somewhat detailed account of the
heroine's youth, her career at school, her first
confession and early marriage, — all these
being preliminary to the impropriety and the
interest of the book, which, after the repre-
hensible manner of French novels, began
together, — I laid down the volume with a
sigh, and resigned myself to a ride of unalle-
viated dulness.

A resource instantly presented itself, however, in the page which the lady in the seat
before me was reading.   As I glanced up I
saw that she was entertaining herself with
poetry, and the next moment a familiar line
caught my eye : —

" If you were April's lady, and I were lord of May."

"Swinburne," I mused, "or a collection of selected poems, perhaps. Wiseacres would say one ought to know what a reader is like by the book she reads; but in the first place that's nonsense, and in the second place I don't know what book she is reading. She has an exquisite ear, and her hair is something bewildering. 'If you were April's lady.' April's lady should be a capricious creature, ⌐all smiles and tears, with winning ways and wilful wiles, — impulsive and wayward, and thoroughly enchanting. It would not," — my thoughts ran on in a professional turn, while my eyes dwelt appreciatively, if somewhat presumptuously, upon the lovely curve of my neighbor's neck, — "it would not be a bad notion to write a story of such a maiden and call it 'April's Lady.' Let me see, what should it be like?"

And upon this impulse I fell to pondering, when suddenly, as if by magic, a tale presented itself all complete in my mind. My mental action appeared to me more like that of remembering than of creating, so real and so complete was the pretty history. The self-willed, volatile damsel whose fortunes it concerned seemed one whom I had known, and whom I might meet again some day. In my mind she assumed, it is true, an outward semblance similar to that of the lady before me, upon whose back I fixed my regards in an absorbed stare, which should have disturbed her could looks make themselves felt. She did not move, however, and as she did not turn the leaf of her book, I fancied she might have fallen into a reverie as deep as my own. I had not been able fully to see her face, although a lucky turn had given me a glimpse of a profile full of character and beauty, and which made me desire to behold more. I did not, however, trouble myself about the exact details of my heroine's features, since every story-teller has a stock of choice personal charms with which to endow his fictitious children, but continued to gloat over my little romance; and so vividly was the tale of "April's Lady" impressed upon my mind that although some weeks elapsed before I found time to put it upon paper, I had not the slightest difficulty in recalling even its most trifling incidents.

Almost the whole of my journey was taken up in turning the story over in my mind, and when we drew into the Boston station, and my neighbor closed her volume to begin the collection of her numerous feminine possessions, I had half a mind to lean forward and thank her for having given me, although unconsciously, so good a story.

It did seem to me, even after I had sent my manuscript off and the dreadful moment came when one realizes that it is too late to make changes and consequently thinks of plenty of things he wishes to alter, that "April's Lady" was the best work I had ever done. I had let a month or two pass between its first writing and the final revision, and I was pretty well satisfied that I had produced a really capital story. I fondly hoped Mr. Lane, the editor of the "Dark Red," would be moved by its excellence to give me further orders; and the eagerness with which I one morning tore open an envelope upon which I recognized his handwriting, may be easily enough imagined, at least by members of the literary guild. My impatience gave place to profound astonishment as I read the following note : —

OFFICE DARK RED MAGAZINE,
BOSTON, September 27.

My DEAR MR. GRAY, — Can you drop into my office to-morrow about noon? By some odd co-incidence I received a story very similar to your "April's Lady," and bearing the same title, several days earlier, and should like to talk with you about it.

Very truly yours,

J. Q. LANE.

I was utterly confounded. I racked my brains to discover who could possibly have stolen my story, and even suspected the small black girl who dusted my rooms, although the sooty little morsel did not know one letter from another. The first draft of the story had lain in my desk for some time, it was true, yet that any literary burglar should have forced an entrance and then contented himself with copying this seemed, upon the whole, scarcely probable. I ransacked my memory for some old tale which I might unconsciously have plagiarized, but I could think of nothing; and, moreover, I reflected that the coincidence of names certainly could not be accounted for in this way, even did I recall the germ of my plot.

I presented myself at the office of the "Dark Red" at the hour appointed with a clear conscience, it is true, but with positively no suggestion whatever to offer in regard to the method by which a copy of my story could have reached the editor in advance of my own manuscript.

Mr. Lane received me with the conventionally cordial manner which is as much a part of editorial duties as is the use of the blue pencil, and without much delay came to the business of the call.

"There is something very singular about this affair," he said, laying out my manuscript, and beside it another which I could see was written in a running feminine hand. "If the stories were a little more alike, I should be sure one was copied from the other; as it is, it is inconceivable that they have not at least a common origin. Where did you get your idea?"

"Why, so far as I know," I replied in perplexity, "I evolved it from my inner consciousness; but the germ may have been the unconscious recollection of some incident or floating idea. I've tried to discover where I did get the fancy, but without a glimmer of success. Who sent you the other version?"

"A lady of whose integrity I am as sure as I am of yours. That's the odd part of it. Besides, you are both of you too clever to plagiarize, even if you were n't too honest. The mere similarity of theme is n't so strange; that happens often enough; but that the title of the stories should be identical, and that in each the heroine should be named May—"

"Is her heroine named May?" I interrupted in astonishment; "why, then, she must have seen my copy; or," I added, a new thought striking me, "she must have got the name in the same way I did. I took the title of the story and the name of the heroine from a line of Swinburne, and — "

" And," interrupted the editor in turn, catching up the manuscript before him, "so did she."

And he showed me, written at the head of the page : —

" If you were April's lady, and I were lord of May."

" Well," I remarked, with a not unnatural mingling of philosophy and anoyance, " it is all of a piece with my theory that ideas are in the air, and belong, like wild geese, to whoever catches them first; but it is vexatious, when I captured a fancy that particularly pleased me, to find that some woman or other has been smart enough to get salt on its tail-feathers before I did."

Mr. Lane smiled at my desperate air, and at that moment his little office-boy, whom I particularly detest because of the catlike stillness and suddenness of his movements, silently produced first himself and then a card.

" ' Agnes Graham,' " read Mr. Lane. " Here is your rival to speak for herself. I hope you don't mind seeing her?"

" Oh, by no means," I replied rather ungraciously. " Let us see what she is like, and what she will have to say about this puzzle."

The name was not wholly new to me,
as I had seen it signed to various magazine
articles, concerning which at this moment I
had only the most vague and general idea.
I was sitting with my back to the door, and
in rising I still kept my face half turned away
from the lady who entered, but I saw the
reflection of her face in a mirror opposite
without any sense of recognition. As she
advanced a step or two, however, and half
passed me, I knew her. The delicate ear, the
fine sweep of the neck, the knot of golden
brown hair, were all familiar. It was the
lady who had sat before me in the cars from
New York on that April day.

As she turned in recognition of Mr. Lane's
introduction, a faint flush seemed to show
that she too recognized me, although I was
unable to understand how she should know
me, since she certainly had not turned her
head once in the entire journey. I set it
down to pure feminine intuition, not having
wholly freed myself from that masculine
superstition which regards woman's instinct
as a sort of supernatural clairvoyance.

My sensations on discovering her identity
were not wholly unlike those of a man who
inadvertently touches a charged Leyden jar.

" Good heavens ! " I exclaimed, " what a

psychological conundrum, or whatever you choose to call it. The whole matter is as plain to me now as daylight."

"Well?" Mr. Lane asked, while Miss Graham regarded me with an air which seemed to question whether my insanity were of a dangerous type.

"Pardon me, Miss Graham, if I cross-question you a little," I went on, becoming somewhat excited. "You came from New York on the morning train on Wednesday, the fifteenth — no, the sixteenth of last April, did you not?"

"Yes," she answered, her color again a trifle heightened, but her appearance being rather that of perplexity than of self-consciousness.

"And on the way you read Swinburne till you came to the line,

‘ If you were April's lady, and I were lord of May,’
and it occurred to you what a capital name for a story ‘ April's Lady’ would be?"

"Yes," she repeated; and then, with a yet more puzzled air, she turned to Mr. Lane to ask, " Is this mind-reading?"

"I'm sure I don't know," returned he. " Mr. Gray can best tell what it is."

"And the rest of the way to Boston," I continued, ignoring the interruption, " you were elaborating your story. You took the heroine's name from the same line, and had a pun at the climax about the hero's becoming ' lord of May.' "

" No," Miss Graham retorted, beginning to enter into the spirit of the situation. " I deny the pun, although I acknowledge the rest. The pun I did n't even think of."

" Well, you see I have n't read your manuscript, but I own I fell so low that I put in the pun myself. At least the old gentleman with a scar on his cheek, who sat in the corner of the car, gave you hints for — "

" The uncle," broke in Miss Graham, with a gleeful laugh at the remembrance of the oddity of the old gentleman's appearance. " But how in the world did you know? "

" Oh, he did me. We evidently had the same mental experience; which proves, I suppose, that we are literary Corsican brothers or something of the sort."

" But the great question to be settled is," Mr. Lane observed, bringing in, after some further talk, the editorial consideration, "whose story this really is."

" Miss Graham's, by all means," I said instantly. " Hers was first in the field, and if I had n't impertinently looked over her shoulder, I should n't have had any share in it whatever."

Miss Graham laughed, showing a delicious dimple, and Mr. Lane, who evidently had no desire to settle the question under discussion, looked inquiringly at her for a response to my words.

"You are very generous, Mr. Gray," she answered; "but in the first place my story has never been accepted for the 'Dark Red,' and in the second, as the stories really ought to stand on their merits, I shall certainly not venture to put mine into competition with yours, but prefer to pocket my manuscript and retire."

"I fear," was my reply, "that I discover rather a tendency to sarcasm in what you say than any true humility. Of course the first point is one for Mr. Lane to settle."

The editor cleared his throat with some embarrassment, but before he found the words he wanted, Miss Graham spoke again.

"I had not the slightest idea of being sarcastic, for, of course, it goes without saying that your story is better than mine; but since you choose to take it in that way, I am willing to leave the whole matter to Mr. Lane. He is at least the only person who has read both manuscripts."

"Really," Mr. Lane said, thus pushed into a corner, "I am extremely sorry to find my-

self placed in so trying a situation. There
are points in which each story excels, and
the best result would undoubtedly be at-
tained by welding them together."

"If that could be done," said Miss Graham,
thoughtfully.

"Now, in Mr. Gray's version," he continued,
"the heroine is more attractive and real."

"That," I interpolated, trying to cover the
awkwardness I felt by a jest, "is the first
time in all my literary experience that the
character I thought best in a story I'd
written has seemed so to the editorial
mind."

The dark eyes of my neighbor gave me a
bright, brief glance, but whether of sympathy
with my statement or of contempt for the
feebleness of my attempts at being jocose, I
could not determine.

"While Miss Graham," went on the editorial comment, "has decidedly the advantage
in her hero."

Miss Graham flushed slightly, but offered
no remark in reply to this opinion beyond a
smile which seemed one of frank pleasure.
We sat in silence a moment, a not unnatural
hesitancy preventing my making a proposition which had presented itself to my
mind.

"If it will not seem impertinent to Miss Graham," I ventured at length, "I would propose that we really do try the experiment of collaboration on this story. I have never worked with anybody, but I promise to be tractable; and the thing had so odd a beginning that it is a pity to thwart the evident intention of destiny that we shall both have a hand in it."

To this proposition the lady at first returned a decided and even peremptory negative; but my persausions, seconded by those of Mr. Lane, who was partly curious and partly anxious to escape from the necessity of arbitrating in the matter, in the end induced her to alter her decision.

The result of the interview was that when we left the office of the " Dark Red " Miss Graham had my manuscript and I hers, and that an appointment had been made for my calling upon her with a view to an interchange of comments and criticisms.

Upon the appointed evening I presented myself at the home of Miss Graham, and al most without the usual conventionalites concerning the weather we proceeded to discuss the stories. We began with great outward suavity and courtesy the exchange of compliments, which were so obviously formal and perfunctory that in a moment more we looked into each other's faces and burst into laughter which if hardly polite was at least genuine.

" Come," I said, " now the ice is broken and we can say what we really think ; and I must be pardoned for saying that that hero of yours, whom Mr. Lane praised, is the most insufferable cad I 've encountered this many a day. He can't be set off against that lovely girl in my story. Why, the truth is, Miss Graham, I meant her to be what I fancied you might be. She 's the ideal I built up from seeing you in the cars."

" I must say," Miss Graham retorted with spirit, " that if you meant that pert heroine of yours for *me*, I am anything but complimented."

." It is a pity, then, that you did n't intend your hero for me, and we should have been more than quits."

She blushed so vividly that a sudden light burst upon me.

" Good heavens ! " I exclaimed, " he does have my eyes and beard ; but you did n't see me. It is n't possible — "

" But it is," interrupted she, desperately. " With a mirror in the end of the car directly before me all the way from New York, do you suppose I could help seeing

you! I'm sure you kept your eyes on me
steadily enough to give me a good excuse."

I whistled rudely; whereat she looked
offended, and we went on from one thing to
another until we had got up a very respect-
able quarrel indeed. There is nothing more
conducive to a thoroughly good understanding between persons of opposite sex than a
genuine quarrel; and having reached the
point where there was no alternative but to
separate in anger or to apologize, we chose
the latter course, and having mutually hum-
bled ourselves, after that got on capitally.

"It is my deliberate conviction," she observed, when we at length got upon a footing
sufficiently familiar for jesting, "that this
story is really mine, and that you purloined it
from me by some mysterious clairvoyance."

"That may be," I admitted. "I once
guessed that a man was a bartender by the
way he stirred his coffee at the steamer table,
and that got me a very pretty reputation as a
seer for a day or two; and very likely the
truth is that I was all the time a mind-reader
without knowing it."

She smiled good-naturedly — more good-
naturedly, indeed, than the jest deserved; and
from that moment our acquaintance got on
famously. The story was far from advancing

as rapidly, however. A very brief time suf-
ficed to reduce both versions of "April's
Lady" to hopeless confusion, but to build
from the fragments a new and improved
copy was a labor of much magnitude. Circumstances moreover, conspired to hinder
our work. It was necessary that we verify
our impressions of material we had used, and
to do this we were obliged to attend the
theatre together, to read together various
poems, and together to hear a good deal of
music. A little ingenuity, and a common
inclination to prolong these investigations,
effected so great a lengthening out that it
was several months before we could even pretend to be ready to begin serious work upon
the story; and even then we were far from
agreeing in a number of important particulars.

"Agnes," I remarked, one February evening, when we were on our way home from a
concert to which we had boldly gone without
even a pretence that it was in the remotest
way connected with our literary project, " I
fear we are becoming demoralized, and it
seems to me the only hope of our ever com-
pleting 'April's Lady' is to put everything
else aside for the time being and give our
minds to it. I can get my work arranged,
and you can finish those articles for 'The

Quill ' by the middle of March. Then, we
can be quietly married and go to some nice
old-fashioned place — say St. Augustine —
for a couple of months and get this *magnum
opus* on paper at last."

"As to being married," returned she se-
dately, " have you considered that we could
not possibly make a living, since we should
inevitably be always writing the same things?"

" Why, that is my chief reason," I retorted,
" for proposing it. Think how awkward it is
going to be if either of us marries somebody
else, and then we write the same things. It
is a good deal better to have our interests in
common if our inventive faculty is to be so."

"There is something in what you say,"
Agnes assented; " and it would be especially
awkward for you, since the invention is in my
head."

" Then we will consider it all arranged."

" Oh, no, George; by no means. I couldn't
think of it for a minute ! "

Whether she did think of it for a minute is
a point which may be left for the settling of
those versed in the· ways of the feminine
mind; certain it is that the programme was
carried out — except in one trifling particular.
We were quietly married, we did go to St.
Augustine, but as for doing anything with

the story, that was quite another thing. We did not finish it then, and we have not finished it yet, and I have ceased to have any very firm confidence that we ever shall finish it; although, whenever arises one of those financial crises which are so painfully frequent in the family of a literary man, and we sit down to consider possible resources, one or the other of us is sure sooner or later to observe : —

"And then there is 'April's Lady,' you know." '

Interlude Eighth.

———◆———

A CUBAN MORNING.

A CUBAN MORNING.

[*Scene, the shady piazza of the hotel at Marianao, Cuba. Time, nine o'clock on a hot March morning. Miss Peltonville and Arthur Chester tête-à-tête.*]

She. Why did you follow us to Cuba?

He. I have already told you that I thought you were in Florida.

She. Yes? And so you came to Marianao, where nobody comes at this time of year, in order that you might be perfectly safe from an encounter, I suppose.

He. Oh, I — that is; precisely.

She. I had a letter from Annie Cleaves yesterday.

He. Had you?

She. Yes; and she said you told her that you were coming to Cuba to find me.

He. Oh, that's nothing. It isn't to be supposed I told her the truth.

She. Do you speak the truth so seldom, then? Is there no dependence to be put on what you say?

He. None whatever; otherwise I should be continually hampered by the necessity of conforming my actions to my words. You can see yourself how inconvenient that would be.

She. For one who has had so little practice, very likely; but then you would find it a novel experience, I have no doubt.

He. Ah, you have given me an idea. I 'll try it when all other novelties in life are exhausted.

She. Don't put it off too long, or from the force of habit you may find it impossible.

He. You underrate my adaptability.

She. Meanwhile I wish to know why you came.

He. Since you are here yourself, you might be supposed to regard the place as sufficiently interesting to attract the traveller.

She. Then you decline to tell me?

He. Oh, no ; I came because you amuse me.

She. Thank you for nothing.

He. And consequently I am in love with you, as I did myself the honor to mention before you left New York.

She. Am I to understand that amusement is your idea of love?

He. Love certainly must be something that does not bore one.

She. But it seems a somewhat limited view to take.

He. Oh, it is only one way out of many; I assure you I have quantities of ideas upon the subject, all founded upon experience. I loved Lottie Greenwell because she made a glorious champagne cup. Indeed, for ten days I positively adored her, until one night she put in too much curaçoa, and I

realized how uncertain a foundation my passion
had. Then there was Elsie Manning. My passion
for her was roused entirely by her divine waltzing,
but I realized that it is n't good form for a man to
waltz with his wife, and I stood a much better chance
if she married some other man. After that came
Kate Turner; she writes so fascinating a letter that
I lost my heart every time I saw her handwriting
on the back of an envelope, although perhaps that
feeling you would call only a fancy, since nobody
would think of marrying on a virtue that is sure to
end with the wedding. A wife never writes to her
husband about anything but the servants and the
payment of her milliner's bills; so my flirtation
with her would n't really count as a love affair.

She. You excel in nice metaphysical distinctions.

He. Then there was Miss French. I loved her
because she snubbed me, — just as I loved Nora
Delaney for her riding, and Annie Cleaves for her
music.

She. And now you love me, I am to understand,
as suited to the position of court jester to your
Royal Highness.

He. One must have some sort of a reason for
being in love.

She. But one need n't be in love.

He. Oh, yes; life is very dull otherwise; and
besides, I have always thought it very stupid to
marry without having been in love a dozen times
at least. One is apt to lose his head otherwise;

and how can he judge of the value of his passion without having had a good deal of experience?

She. So you advertise yourself as a marrying man?

He. Every bachelor is a marrying man. It is only a question of finding a convenient wife.

She. Like a convenient house, I suppose.

He. Exactly.

She. I wonder any woman ever consents to marry a man.

He. They know their own sex too well to be willing to marry a woman.

She. But men are such selfish creatures!

He. You are amazingly pretty when you toss your head that way. It is worth coming from New York to see.

She. It is well you think so; otherwise you might consider your voyage a waste of time.

He. What, with the certainty of your consenting to marry me?

She. I like your assurance! Why should I marry you?

He. I supposed that with your sex the fact of my amazing attachment would be a sufficient reason.

She. Your knowledge of our sex is then remarkably limited. Apparently, whether I happen to love you is of no particular consequence.

He. Oh, love is said to beget love.

She. But you love me, you say, because I amuse

you. Now you don't amuse me in the least, and as I do not know just how to cultivate a passion simply on the rather doubtful ground of your affection, especially with the chance of its being transient, there really seems to be very little chance of reciprocity.

He. Do you know what a tremendously hot day it is?

She. I don't see the connection, and I am sure I am cool enough.

He. But you make it very hot for me! How picturesque that ragged fellow over there looks, riding on the top of his high saddle.

She. With a string of mules tied to his horse's tail. I am fond of the mules, their bells are so musical.

He. And their bray.

She. And the muleteers sing such weird songs. I hear them going by about four o'clock in the morning, on their way to the Havana market, and the effect is most fascinating.

He. I should have expected you to be fond of the mules.

She. Why?

He. A fellow feeling is said to have a softening effect, and the mule's strongest characteristic is —

She. Consistency!

He. And as I was about to remark, we are apt to value others most for the virtues we do not ourselves possess.

She. You are sufficiently rude.

He. There is always danger that honesty will be thought rude.

She. Really, you begin to amuse me. Please go on; I would like to try falling in love on the amusement plan; it must be very droll.

He. Oh, bother the amusement! Like the young ladies in novels, I would be loved for myself alone.

She. I fear that would be more difficult than the other way. What have you ever done to make me admire you?

He. Perhaps nothing. Admiration presupposes the capability of appreciation.

She. Ah! What have you done, then, worthy of admiration?

He. I have managed to find you at Marianao, and bring about a tête-à-tête before I have been here fifteen hours.

She. Wonderful man! And of all that, what comes?

He. That I ask you to marry me. That is certainly something.

She. Yes; it is n't much, and you have done it before. But as you say, it is certainly something.

He. You are always flattering! Really, one would n't have expected you to be light now, when it is my deepest affections and all that sort of touching thing with which you are trifling.

She. You are a humbug!

He. Of course; so are you; so is everybody. Civilization is merely the apotheosis of humbug.

She. My friend, that trick of striving after epigram is fast making you as bad as a confirmed punster.

He. Still, it is all true. I am a humbug in proposing to you; you, if you reject me —

She. I certainly do, most emphatically and finally !

He. You make me the happiest of men.

She. You make your system of humbug far too complicated for me to follow.

He. Why, this is genuine.

She. Anything genuine from you, I fear, is impossible.

He. Oh, no; I have to be genuine occasionally, for the sake of contrast. The humbug was in asking you to marry me, and I would n't have had you say yes for the world.

She. I never suspected you of insanity, Mr. Chester. Am I to infer that the climate of Cuba, or the wines —

He. Oh, neither, I assure you. Besides, Cuba has no wines, as you ought to know. Now, see; I 'll do you the rare honor of telling you the truth. Of course, you are at liberty to believe it or not, as you please; and very likely you won't, because it happens to be as true as the Gospel, revised version. Some days since, I asked Annie Cleaves to marry me.

She. What particular thing had she been playing to rouse you to that point of enthusiasm?

He. If my memory serves me, it was the Chopin Nocturne in G minor. She did play extremely well, and as we happened to be in the conservatory afterward, I improved the opportunity to propose.

She. Oh, very naturally!

He. It is a form of words that comes very readily to my lips, as you know. Annie confessed to that very superfluous and old-fashioned sentiment called love, which was n't in good form, I 'll admit; but in consideration for the object of her attachment, and the fact that on that particular evening I was in love myself, I managed to overlook it.

She. Very good of you, I 'm sure. I hope Annie appreciated your generosity.

He. Very likely she did n't. Your sex very seldom do appreciate masculine virtues; but Annie has a far more old-fashioned and worse vice than love. Why, the girl, in the midst of these enlightened nineteenth-century days, actually goes to the nonsensical bother of keeping a conscience! It must be more trouble to attend to, Agnes, than her aunt Wheeler's seven pet poodles and three red-headed parrots.

She. I suppose you are right. You don't speak from experience, though, do you?

He. Oh, no; I never had a conscience: as a boy, I preferred white mice; now I have my horses, you know.

She. And your innumerable loves.

He. If such trifles are to be taken into account.

She. Go on about Annie.

.He. Well, on my confessing how far I had carried my flirtation with you — I can't, for the life of me, tell how I happened to speak of it; I am usually more discreet.

She. I should hope so.

He. Oh, I am, I assure you; but the loves are so numerous, while I am but one, that they sometimes get the better of my discretion. What is one among so many?

She. Oh, in this case, absolutely nothing.

He. Thank you again.

She. But to continue —

He. Well, to continue, Annie actually seemed to think that you had some sort of claim upon me. Fancy!

She. She need n't have troubled.

He. Oh, of course not. Why, I have offered myself to dozens of girls, with no more idea of marrying them than I have of becoming a howling dervish; and more than that, I have habitually been accepted. That is one thing about you that attracted me, do you know? There is a beautiful novelty about being rejected.

She. So that is the secret of my amusing you, is it? You ought to have explained this to Annie.

He. Oh, she would n't have understood. Like every other girl, 't was the personal application that she was touched by. You see she did n't know the other girls, and she did know you ; and she seems to think your no more binding than any other person's yes. Perhaps she knows that a woman's negative —

She. Really, Arthur, that 's so hackneyed that if you have n't the gallantry not to say it you ought to be ashamed to repeat anything so stale.

He. Perhaps you are right ; I have known you to be on very rare occasions. However, Annie insisted that I should come, and, as she said, "assure myself of your sentiments and of my own." Did you ever hear anything more absurd ? As if I did n't know, all the time, that you were dying for me ; and as if I — despite my mad and overpowering passion for your lovely self, Miss Peltonville — could n't tell as well in New York as in Cuba whether I wanted to marry her or not.

She. If you were no better informed of your own sentiments than of mine, I don't wonder she doubted your conclusions.

He. Oh, she did n't in the least.

She. At least, Annie may set her mind quite at rest, so far as I am concerned.

He. Thank you so much. It is such a relief to have things settled.

She. What would you have done if I had accepted you ?

He. Oh, I was confident of my ability of putting the question so that you would n't.

She. I have almost a mind to do it, even now.

He. Really?

She. Oh, don't be alarmed. There is one insuperable obstacle.

He. What is that?

She. Yourself.

He. Then I am quite safe. That is a permanent one.

She. Well, I wish Annie joy of her bargain. She is worthy of a better fate; and since we are talking frankly, I must say that what she can see in you I can't imagine.

He. These things are so strange; there is no accounting for them. Why, I have been perfectly puzzled — do you know? — ever since I came last night, to tell what I found in you last winter.

She. Since we seem to be striving to outdo each other in abuse, it is quite in keeping for me to add, that I have no occasion to bother my head on such a question, for I never pretended to have found anything in you.

He. But then, as I said, you amused me; and one may sometimes be so far amused that —

She. His amusement may even amount to astonishment, perhaps; and, by the way, that gentleman on the gray horse, just coming between the China laurels with papa, expects to marry me.

He. Fred Armstrong, by all that is unspeakable! Agnes Peltonville, I humble myself in the dust before you; and no humiliation could be greater than going down into Cuban dust. You are an angel; you have removed my last fear.

She. Yes; and how?

He. I was always jealous of Fred Armstrong; he was forever dangling about Annie. Do I understand that you are engaged?

She. Oh, I did n't say that I expected to marry him; but since Annie confesses such a strong attachment to you —

He. Oh, I did n't say I was the object of the attachment.

[*They sit confronting each other in silence a moment, until the riders, having dismounted, are seen approaching the piazza. Then Chester leans forward impulsively, and speaks with a new intensity.*]

He. Agnes!

She. Arthur!

He. Quick! Before they come! You won't send me away?

She. But —

He. No, no more nonsense; I am in dead earnest now. You know I could n't live without you, or I should n't have followed you to Cuba.

She. And Annie Cleaves?

He. Oh, if you had a letter from her yesterday, you must know she 's engaged to Bob Wainwright. Is it yes?

She. (*rising.*) It would be a pity that you should have come so far for nothing.

[*As he rises also he manages to catch her hand, which he clasps joyously before the pair go forward to meet the new-comers.*]

He. I hope you had a pleasant ride, Mr. Peltonville? I like Marianao so well that I have concluded to remain a while.

Tale the Ninth.

———◆———

DELIA GRIMWET.

DELIA GRIMWET.

O an ordinary observer, nothing could be more commonplace than Kempton, a decrepit little apology for a village, lying on the coast of Maine. Properly speaking, however, no seaport can be utterly commonplace, with its suggestion of the mystery of the sea, the ships, the sailors who have been to far lands, the glimpses of unwritten tragedies on every hand. But among sea-side villages Kempton was surely dull enough, and dry enough, and lifeless enough, — as if the sea-winds had sucked its vitality, leaving it empty and pallid and juiceless, like the cockle-shells which bleached upon its sandy beaches.

Yet Kempton had one peculiarity which marked it as singular among all New England towns. It had a woman to dig its graves.

Its one church stood stark and doleful upon the hill at whose foot lay the rotting wharves; and back from the church stretched the church-yard in which the Kempton dead took their long repose, scarcely more monotonous than their colorless lives. The sexton, digging their last resting-places in the ochery loam, might look far off toward the sea where they had wrested from the grudging waters a scanty subsistence; and the dead wives, if so be that their ears were yet sentient, might lie at night and hear below the beat of the waves which afar had rolled over the un-marked graves of their sailor husbands.

To and fro among the grass-grown mounds the sexton went daily, quite unmindful of be-ing the unique feature of Kempton by be-longing to the weaker sex. With masculine stride and coarse hands, her unkempt locks blown by the salt winds, the woman went her way and did her work with a steadfastness and a vigor which might have put to shame many a man idling about the boats under the hill. She was not an old woman, — not even middle-aged, except with the premature age of toil and sorrow; but the weather-beaten face, the stooping shoulders, and the faded hair made her seem old. To look at her, it was difficult to realize what her youth could have been like, or to call up any image of sweet or gracious maidenhood in which she could have shared.

It was a gray November day. The white-caps made doubly black the dark waves of

the bay, and the bitter wind blew freshly
through the withered grass and stubble, chas-
ing the faded leaves over Kempton Hill until
they rushed about the old meeting-house like
a flight of terrified witches. A stranger was
driving slowly up the road from the next
town in an open carriage, and as he came to
the top of the hill he drew rein before the
church and looked about him.

His gaze was not that of one who beheld
the scene for the first time. He gazed down
at the irregular houses under the hill, cuddled
like frightened and weak-kneed sheep. He
looked over the bay to the lighthouse, loom-
ing ghastly and white against the dark sea
and sky. His glance took in all the details
of the picture, cold and joyless, devoid alike
of warmth and color. He shivered and
sighed, his brows drooping more heavily yet
over his dark piercing eyes, and then turned
his gaze to objects nearer at hand.

Close by was the stark church, with
weather-beaten steeple, wherein half a dozen
generations of Kempton women, — the men,
for the most part, being at sea, — had worshipped the power of the storm, praying
more for the escape from evil of the absent
than for good to themselves. Beyond the
church appeared the first headstones of the

graveyard, the ground sloping away so rapidly that little more than the first row of slate
slabs was visible from the street. With another shiver Mr. Farnsworth (for by that
name the gentleman played his part upon
this world's stage) got down from his carriage, fastened his horse, and walked toward
the stones, whose rudely chiselled cherubs
leered at him through their tawny rust of
moss with a diabolic and sinister mirthfulness.

As Mr. Farnsworth opened the sagging
and unpainted gate of the enclosure, he became aware that the place was not empty.
The head and shoulders of a human being
were visible half-way down the hill, now and
then obscured by the dull-reddish heap of
earth thrown up from a partially dug grave.

The visitor made his way down the irregular path, so steep as to be almost like a rude
flight of stairs, and as he neared the worker,
he suddenly perceived, with something of a
shock, that the grave-digger was a woman.
She worked as if familiar with her task, a
man's battered hat pushed back from her
forehead, over which her faded hair straggled
in confusion, and across which certain grimy
streaks bore witness that she had not escaped
the primal curse, but labored in the sweat of
her brow.

Kempton's peculiarity in the matter of its
sexton had not come to the knowledge of the
stranger before, although he once had known
the village life somewhat intimately. He regarded the woman with a double curiosity, —
to see what she was like and to discover
whether perchance he had ever known her.
He paused as he neared her, resting one
nicely gloved hand upon a tilted stone which
perpetuated the memory and recorded the
virtues of a captain who reposed in some
chill cave under the Northern seas. Some
slight sound caught the ear of the sexton,
who until then had not perceived his approach; she looked up at him stolidly, and
as stolidly looked down again, continuing her
work without interruption. If there remained
any consciousness of the strangeness of
her occupation, or if there stirred any womanly shame to be so observed, they were
betrayed by no outward sign. She threw up
the dull-yellow earth at the feet of the new-
comer as unmoved as if she had still only the
dwellers in the graves as companions of her
labor.

"Don't you find this rather hard work,
my good woman?" the gentleman inquired
at length, more by way of breaking the silence than from any especial interest.

"Yes," the sexton returned impassively, "it's hard enough."

"It is rather unusual work for a woman. too," he said.

To this very obvious remark she returned no answer, a stone to which she had come in her digging seeming to absorb all her attention. She unearthed the obstacle with some difficulty, seized it with her rough hands, and threw it up at the feet of the stranger, who watched her with that idle interest which labor begets in the unconcerned observer.

"Do you always do this work?" Farnsworth asked at length.

"Yes," was the laconic return.

"But the old sexton, — Joe Grimwet, — is he gone?"

The woman looked up with some interest at this indication that the other had some previous acquaintance with Kempton and its people. She did not, however, stop her labor, as a man would probably have stopped.

"Yes," she said. "He's buried over yonder, — there beyond the burdocks."

The gentleman changed his position uneasily. Some subtile disquietude had arisen to disturb his serenity. The wind rustled mournfully among the dry leaves, the pebbles rattled against the spade of the grave-

digger, increasing the sombreness of a scene
which might easily affect one at all suscepti-
ble to outward influences. In such an atmosphere a sensitive nature not unfrequently experiences a certain feeling of unreality, as if
dealing with scenes and creatures of the imagination rather than with actualities; and
Farnsworth, whatever the delicacy of his
mental fibre, was conscious of such a sense
at this moment. He hastened to speak again,
as if the sound of his own voice were needed
to assure him of the genuineness of the place
and scene.

"But how long has he been dead?" he
asked. "And his daughter; what became of
her?"

The grave-digger straightened herself to
her full height; brushing back her wind-
blown hair with one grimy hand, she raised
her face so that her deep-set eyes were fixed
upon the questioner's face.

"So you knew Delia Grimwet?" she said.
"When was you here before? It'd go hard
for you to make her out now, if it's long
since."

"Is she here still?" Farnsworth persisted,
ignoring her question.

"Yes," the sexton replied, suddenly sinking back into the unfinished grave as a

frightened animal might retreat into its den. " Yes ; she lives in the old place."

" Alone ? "

" Her and the boy."

He recoiled a step, as if the mention of a child startled or repelled him. Yet to a close observer it might have seemed as if he were making an effort to press her with further questions. If so his courage did not prove sufficient, and he watched in silence while the woman before him went steadily on with her arduous work. Presently, however, he advanced again toward the edge of the pit, which was rapidly approaching completion under her familiar labor.

" Should I find her at home at this time? " he inquired. " Or would she be out at work ? "

The woman started and crouched, much as if she had received or expected a blow.

" She 's out, most likely," she replied in a muffled voice. " She 'll be home along about sundown."

Farnsworth lingered irresolutely a moment or two, as if there were many things concerning which he could wish to ask ; but, as the woman gave him no encouragement, he turned at last and climbed the slippery, ragged path up to the church, untethered his.

horse, and drove slowly down the hill to the village.

Cap'n Nat Hersey was just coming out of the village store, and to him Farnsworth addressed an inquiry where he might find shelter for himself and horse.

"Well," the cap'n responded, with the deliberation of a man who has very little to say and his whole life to say it in, "well I dunno but ye might get a chance with Widder Bemis, an' I dunno *as* ye could; but there ain't no harm trying, as I knows of."

Further inquiry regarding the whereabouts of the domicile of the Widow Bemis led to an offer on the part of Cap'n Hersey to act as pilot to that haven. He declined, however, to take a seat in the buggy. The Cap'n had his own opinion of land-vehicles. A man might with perfect assurance trust himself in a boat; but, for his own part, the cap'n had no faith in those dangerous structures which roam about with nothing better than dry land under them. He walked along by the side of the carriage, conversing affably with the stranger under his convoy.

"Isn't it a queer notion to have a woman for a sexton?" Farnsworth asked, as they wended along.

"Well, yes," the captain returned reflect-

ively.. "Yes, it is sort of curious. Folks
mostly speaks of it that comes here. It is
curious, if ye look at it that way. But it all
come about as natural as a barnacle on a
keel. Old Sexton Grimwet kept getting considerable feeble, and Dele she took to help-
ing him with his work. She was sort of cut
off from folks, as ye may say, owing to having a baby and no father to show for it, and
she naturally took to heaving anchor alone,
or leastways along with the old man. And
when the old man was took down with a lan-
guishment, she turned to and did all his work
for him, — having gradually worked into it,
as you may say."

The cap'n paused to recover from his astonishment at having been betrayed into so
long a speech; but, as the stranger had the
air of expecting him to continue, he presently
went on again:

"There was them that wanted her turned
out when old Grimwet died. Some said a
woman of that character had n't ought to have
no connection with the church, even to digging its graves. But Parson Eaton he was
good for 'em — I 've always noticed that when
these pious men gets their regular mad up
they most generally have things their own
way; and he preached 'em a sermon about

the Samaritan woman, and Mary Magdalene,
and a lot more of them disreputable Scripture
women-folks, and, though he never mentioned
Dele by name, they all knew what he was driving at, and they wilted. 'Twas a pitiful sight
to see the girl a-digging her own father's grave
up there. Me and Tom Tobey and Zenas
Faston took hold and finished it for her."

They moved on in silence a moment or
two. Farnsworth's gaze was fixed upon the
darkening bay, and no longer interrogated his
companion; but the latter soon again took
up his narrative: —

" 'Twas well the parson stood up for Dele,
too; women-folks is so cussed hard on each
other. They would n't ha' let the girl live, I
believe. I always were of the notion there
warn 't no harm in Dele. Some —— city chap
got the better of her. She never was over-
smart, but she was awful pretty; and I never
believed there was any harm in her. At any
rate, she digs a grave as well as a man, and
I guess them that 's in 'em don't lay awake
none thinking who tucked 'em in."

The house of the Widow Bemis was by
this time reached, and that estimable lady,
who in the summer furnished accomodations
to a boarder whenever that rare blessing was
to be secured in Kempton, readily undertook

the charge of Mr. Farnsworth and his horse
for the night. The latter was given into the
care of her daughter, for the frequent ab-
sences of the men had accustomed the damsels of Kempton to those labors which in in-
land villages are more frequently left to their
brothers; and Farnsworth strolled off toward
the wharves, leaving the widow Bemis and
Cap'n Hersey in an agony of curiosity in regard to himself and his errand.

Whatever may have been Farnsworth's
feelings at the discovery that the daughter of
the dead sexton and the woman of whom
he had asked tidings of her were identical, —
and they must have been both deep and
strong — he had given no outward sign. But
now the settling of his brows, and the disquiet
apparent in his eyes betrayed his inward con-
flict. He strolled out upon one of the rotting
wharves about which the tide lapped in
mournful iteration, folded his arms upon a
breast-high post, and stood gazing seaward.

The retrospect which occupied his mind
was scarcely more cheerful than the gray
scene which spread before his eyes. How
awful are the corpses of dead sins which
memory casts up, as the sea its victims!
The betrayal of a woman is a ghastly thing
when one looks back upon it stripped of the

garlands and enchantments of passion and temptation; and to Farnsworth, with the image fresh in his remembrance of that faded, earth-stained woman digging a grave upon the bleak hillside, the fault of his youth seemed an incredible dream which only stubborn and stinging memory converted into a possibility. A retrospect is apt to be essentially a plea for self against conscience; but in his gloomy revery Farnsworth found scant excuse for the wreck he had made of the life of Delia Grimwet. He had gone away, married, and lived honored and prosperous. He would have forgotten, had not some nobility of his nature prevented. With the stubbornness of his race, he had fought long and determinedly against his conscience, but he had been forced to yield at last. The death of his wife, to whom he had been tenderly attached, had at once left him free to make such reparation as might still be possible, and had softened him as only sharp sorrow can. He had come to Kempton with the determination of finding Delia, and of doing whatever could be done, at whatever cost to himself.

He had been unprepared, however, for the woman he found. He had left a fresh, beautiful young girl; ten years had transformed

her into a repulsive old woman. He had no
means of adequately measuring the force of
the storms of scorn and poverty and sorrow
which had beaten upon Delia Grimwet in the
years that had made of him the cultured,
delicately nurtured man he was. What man
ever appreciated the woe of the woman he
betrays? Indeed, what measure has a man
of the sorrow of any woman? Farnsworth
had painfully to adjust himself to a condition
of affairs for which he should have been prepared, yet which took him absolutely by
surprise.

He lingered upon the bleak wharf, unconsciously the object of much mildly specula-
tive curiosity, until the twilight began to fall.
Then with a shiver, no less of mind than of
body, he shook off his painful abstraction,
and turned his steps toward the path, once
well known, which led to the house of Delia
Grimwet. It seemed to him, as he paused a
brief instant with his hand upon the old
knocker, as if nothing here had changed in ten
years. The sunlight would have shown him
traces of decay, but in the gathering dusk
the house seemed a pallid phantom from the
past, unchanged but lifeless.

But his knock at once destroyed all illu-
sions, since it summoned the woman who

belonged not at all to that past which he re-membered, but to the pitiful and too tangible present. She held her guttering candle up without a word, and, having identified him, made him, without speaking, a signal to enter.

When Farnsworth had left her in the after-noon, Delia crouched in the bottom of the grave she was digging, her first feeling being an unreasoning desire for concealment. She thought she should remain passive if the sides of the pit collapsed and buried her. In the old days before her boy was born she had been night after night out on the old wharves, praying for courage to drown herself. After the child came, her feelings changed, and she longed only to escape and to take her son away from the scorn and the sordid life which sur-rounded them. Gradually she had become hardened; hers was one of those common natures to which custom and pain are opiates, mercifully dulling all sensibilities. To-day the appearance of her betrayer had revivified all the old impressions, and for a moment seemed to transport her to the early days when her anguish was new. The keenest pangs of sorrow stabbed her afresh, and she lived again the bitter moments of her sin and shame. Her instinct was to flee from the man whose presence meant to her only pain.

But habit is strong, and presently the fading light reminded the sexton that her work was still unfinished, and that Widow Pettigrove, who was past all earthly tribulation, must have her last bed prepared, whatever the woe of the living woman who worked at it with trembling hands and a sensation as if a demon had clutched her by the throat. Yet work was not unmerciful; it brought some relief, since it served to dilute the thought which rushed dizzyingly to her brain, and by the time her toil was completed she was steadier. When she opened the door to Farnsworth she was not unlike her usual stolid self. She perceived at a glance that he had learned who she was, and she hoped in a blind, aching way, that he had not betrayed his presence to the neighbors, thus to re-awaken all the old stinging flight of bitter words.

Farnsworth followed Delia into the kitchen, without even those greetings which habit renders so involuntary that only in the most poignant moments are they disregarded. With their past between them it was not easy to break the silence. Farnsworth seated himself, and the woman stood regarding him. There was in her attitude all the questioning, all the agony, of her years of suffering. Her wrongs and her sorrows gave her a dignity before which he shrank as he could not have quailed under the most withering reproaches. Whatever words he would have spoken — and no man can come deliberately to so important a crisis without formulating, even if unconsciously, the plea which his self-defence will make — were forgotten, or seemed miserably inadequate now. What were words to this woman, pallid and worn before her time with privation, anguish, and unwomanly toil? The contrast between his rich and careful dress and her coarse garb, between his white hands and her knotted fingers, between his high-bred, pale face and her cowed, weather-beaten countenance, was too violent not to be apparent to them both, — as if they were in some strange way merely spectators looking dispassionately at this wretched meeting of those who had once been passionate lovers.

With each moment the silence became more oppressive; yet as each moment dragged by it became more difficult to break the stillness. Only a man utterly devoid of remorse or feeling could have framed upon his tongue commonplace phrases at such a time. It seemed to Farnsworth as if he were brought to judgment before the whole universe. His throat became parched. He

longed to have the candle and the flames
flickering in the old fireplace go out in darkness, and take from his sight the Nemesis
that confronted him.

He broke the silence at last with a cry: —

"Ah, my God, Delia! What have I
done?"

She wavered as she stood, putting out her
hand as if reaching for support. Then she
half staggered backward into a chair.

"There is nothing I can say!" Farnsworth
went on vehemently. "There is nothing I
can do! I came here dreaming of making
reparation; but there is no reparation I can
make. There is nothing that can change the
past, — nothing that will undo what I have
done to you. Oh, my God! How little I
dreamed it would be like this!"

"No," she said slowly, almost stupidly,
"nothing can undo it."   .

"Why did you not tell me?" he began.
"Why —"

But the words rebuked him before they
were spoken. He buried his face in his
hands, and again they were silent. What
the woman, — this woman who had never
been able to think much, even in her best
days, and who now was blunted and dulled
almost to stupidity, — what she felt in those

bitter moments, who can tell? The man's soul was a tumult of wild regret and unavailing remorse, while she waited again for him to speak.

"But," Farnsworth said at length, a new idea seizing him, "but the — our child, Delia? The boy?"

A shuddering seized her. Unused to giving way to her emotions, she was torn by her excited feelings almost to the verge of convulsions. She clutched the arms of her chair and set her teeth together. In her incoherent attempts at thought, as she had delved among her graves, there had occurred to her the possibility that the father might sometime take his child from her. Now this fear possessed her like a physical epilepsy. Twice she tried to speak, and only emitted a gurgling sound as if strangling. He sprang toward her, but a sudden repulsion gave her self-control. She put out her hands as if to ward him off.

"Oh, my boy, my boy!" she cried, breaking out into hysterical sobs. "My boy, my boy!"

She wrung her hands, and twisted them together in fierce contortions which frightened Farnsworth; but she still would not allow him to approach her. She struggled for composure, writhing in paroxysms dreadful to see.

"Oh, my child!" she cried out, in a tone new and piercing; "no, no! not him! Oh, God! You cannot have my boy!"

Farnsworth retreated sharply.

He had not considered this. Indeed, so different was everything he found from everything he had expected, that whatever he had preconsidered was swept out of existence as irrelevant. He was confronted with a catastrophe in which it was necessary to judge unerringly and to act instantly, yet which paralyzed all his powers by its strangeness and its horror. He groped his way back to his chair and sat down, leaving the silence again unbroken save by her convulsive breathing and his deep-drawn sighs.

All at once a new sound broke in upon them, and the mother started to her feet.

"He is coming!" she gasped hoarsely. "I sent him away; but he has come back. He could not keep away, my beautiful boy."

Her face was illumined with a love which wellnigh transfigured it. The door was opened violently, and the boy came rudely in, — a gaunt, rough whelp of a dozen summers, defiant, bold, and curious.

"I knew there was something up," the

young rascal observed with much self-com-
placency. "I knew when you sent me off
to stay all night that somebody's funeral was
comin' off, and I was bound I'd be here to
see it."

Neither the mother nor the father returned
any answer. Ordinary feelings were so absolutely swept away that the woman did not
even remember that she should have attempted to quiet and to excuse the intruder.
Even the maternal pride which would usually
have been troubled by the impression the
child's rudeness must make upon her guest
was overwhelmed by the greater emotion
which possessed her whole being. ·

Farnsworth had never been more keenly
alive in every fibre of his being than at this
moment. All his family pride, his refined
tastes, his delicate nature, revolted from a
kinship with the ugly, uncouth child who
stood grinning maliciously upon his guilty
parents. His impulse, almost too strong to
be resisted, was to turn back and hide himself
again in the world from which he had come,
— to leave this woman and her loutish child
in the quiet and obscurity in which he had
found them. But he was nobler than his
impulses and had paid already too dearly for
rashness; the claim of a son upon the father

who has brought him into the world grasped his sense of justice like a hand of steel.

He rose to his feet firm and determined.

"Go away now," he said to the boy quietly, but in a voice which even the urchin felt admitted of no disobedience. "I wish to talk with your mother. I will see you to-morrow."

"Yes, Farnsworth," the mother said pleadingly. "Go to bed now. I will come to you before long. That's a good boy."

The boy slowly and unwillingly withdrew, his reluctance showing how rare obedience was to him, and the parents were once more alone.

"You have given him my name," were Farnsworth's first words, as the door closed behind his son.

"It was father who did that. He said he should remember to curse you every time the name was spoken."

"And you?" the other asked, almost with a shudder.

"I did not care. Cursing could not change things. Only I would not let him do it before the boy. I didn't want him to know what sort of a father he had."

In the midst of his self-abasement some hidden fibre of resentment and wounded vanity tingled at her words; but he would not heed it.

" I am not so wholly bad, Delia," he said in a moment. " I came back to marry you. It will not change or mend the past; but it is the best I can do now."

" It is no use to talk of that," she returned wearily; " you and I are done with each other. Even I can see that."

She was spent with the violence of her emotions, and only longed to have Farnsworth leave her. She was keenly sensitive now of the nicety of his attire, the contrast between him and her meagre surroundings. The shamefacedness of the poor overwhelmed her. She rose with uneven steps and trembling hands, and began to put things to rights a little. She snuffed the ill-conditioned candle, and trimmed the fire, whose drift-wood sent out tongues of colored flame. She set back into their usual gaunt and vulgar order the chairs which had been disturbed.

Farnsworth watched her with an aching heart.

" Delia," he said at length, " come and sit down. We must decide what it is best to do."

She obeyed him, although with evident reluctance. All the brief dignity which her elevation of mood had imparted had vanished now, leaving her more haggard and worn than ever. A faded, prematurely old woman, she sat twisting her red, stained hands in a vain attempt to hide their ugliness in the folds of her poor dress. Even self-pity in Farnsworth's breast began to vanish in the depth of compassion which the sexton excited.

"Delia," he said, "I must think for us both, and for the boy. He must be considered. For his sake we must be married.".

It was at once with a sense of relief and of humiliation that he saw how she shrank from this proposition. To have fallen from godhood in the meanest woman's eyes is the keenest thrust at man's pride. It gave Farnsworth a new conception that the gulf between them must look as impassable from her side as from his. He had thus far been too much absorbed in the sacrifices he himself was making to consider that all the desirabilities of his world would not appeal to her as to him, — that its very fulness and richness which so held and delighted him would confuse and repel her.

"It is of no use!" he exclaimed, starting up. "I must have time to think. I will come back in the morning. Think yourself, Delia, — not of me, or even of yourself, so much as of the boy. It is of him that we must have the first care. Nothing can much

change our lives; but the world is before
him. Good-night."

However different may have been the re-
flexions of Farnsworth and of Delia Grimwet
through that long, sad night, their conclusions
must have been in some respects identical,
for when the former came to the house in the
morning with the astonished clergyman the
woman acquiesced without any discussion in
the performance of the marriage ceremony.
It was an occasion which the Rev. Mr.
Eaton long remembered, and of which he
told to the end of his life, filling out, it must
be confessed, as time went on, its spare facts
with sundry incidents, trifling, it is true,
yet gradually overlaying the bare truth with
a completeness which the clerical gossip himself, whose belief always kept pace with his
invention, was far from realizing. The only
thing he could with accuracy have told, beyond the simple fact of the marriage, was that
when, according to his wont, he attempted to
add a few words of exhortation and moral reflection, the bridegroom cut him short and
showed him to the door with a courtesy
perfect but irresistible, the rebuff somewhat
softened by the liberality of the fee which
accompanied the dismissal.

The boy during these singular proceedings

had remained in a state of excited astonishment almost amounting to stupefaction; but
when the newly united family were alone together, his natural perversity broke out, and
showed itself in its natural and unamiable
colors. To the father the child's every uncouth word and act were the most acute
torture; and the mother, partly by woman's
instinct, partly from previous acquaintance
with her husband's fastidiousness, was to
a great degree sensible of this. She made
no effort, however, to restrain her child. She
seemed to have thrown off all responsibility
upon the father, and busied herself in prepar-
ations for the boy's departure, about which,
although neither had spoken of it, there
seemed to be some tacit understanding.

The forenoon was well worn when Farnsworth came to the door with his carriage, for
which he had gone in person.

" Come, Delia," he said, entering the house.
" We may as well leave everything as it is. I
told Mrs. Bemis to lock up the house and
see to it. Are you ready? "

" Farnsworth is," she replied, seating herself in a low chair and drawing to her side the
uncouth boy, who struggled to get free.

He broke in rudely, announcing his readi-
ness, his joy at leaving Kempton, and his sat-

isfaction at wearing his Sunday jacket, which
to his father looked poor enough.

"But you, Delia?" her husband inquired,
putting up his hand to quiet the child. "Are
you ready?"

"I am not going."

Whether it was relief, remorse, or astonishment which overwhelmed him, John
Farnsworth could not have told. He stood
speechless, looking at his wife like one suddenly stricken dumb. The boy filled in the
pause with noisy expostulations, depriving
the tragedy of even the poor dignity of silence. The father knew from the outset that
remonstrances would not be likely to avail,
yet he remonstrated; perhaps, for human
nature is subtle beyond word, he was unconsciously for that reason the more earnest in
his pleading. He would have been glad
could this woman and her child have been
swept out of existence. Already he had to
hold himself strongly in check, lest the reaction which had followed his heroic resolve
to marry Delia should show itself; but
he choked back the feeling with all his
resolution.

"No," Delia persistently said, her eyes dry,
her voice harsh from huskiness. "I've no
place anywhere but here. It is too late now.

I've more feeling than I thought, for I do care something even now to be an honest woman in the sight of my neighbors; and that 'll help me bear it, I suppose. Take the boy, and do for him all you owed to me. I should spoil all if I went. He is best quit of me if he's to please you and grow like you. I'll stay here and dig graves; I am fit for nothing else. I want nothing of you. I married you for the boy's sake, and for his sake I break my heart and send him away; but I will have nothing for myself. The days when I would have taken a penny from you are long gone."

She spoke calmly enough, but with a certain poignant stress which made every word fall like a weight. He did not urge her further. He held out his hand, into which she laid hers lifelessly.

" Good-bye," he said. " As God sees me, Delia, I 'll do my best by the boy. I will write to you. If you change your decision, — but no matter now. I will write to you and to the minister."

All other words of parting were brief and soon spoken. The boy showed no emotion at leaving his mother, as he had throughout exhibited no tenderness. He climbed noisily into the carriage, and the father and son, so

strangely assorted, rode together up the hill,
past the stark meeting-house, and so on into
the world whose seething waves seldom
troubled, even by such a ripple as the events
just narrated, the dull calm of Kempton;
and to John Farnsworth it was as if the woful burden of remorse which had so long
vexed heart and conscience had taken bodily
shape and rode by his side.

Delia had been calm until the two were
gone, — so calm that her husband thought
her still half dazed by the excitement and
anguish of the previous night. She stood
steadily at the window until the carriage
disappeared behind the grave-covered hill.
Then she threw herself grovelling upon the
floor in the very ecstasy of woe. She did
not shriek, strangling in her throat into inarticulate moans and gurglings the cries which
rent their way from her inmost soul; but she
beat her head upon the bare floor; she
caught at the furniture like a wild beast,
leaving the print of her strong teeth in the
hard wood; she was convulsed with her
agony, a speechless animal rage, a boundless,
irrepressible anguish which could not be
measured or expressed. She clutched her
bosom with her savage hands, as if she
would tear herself in pieces; she wounded

and bruised herself with a fierceness so intense as to be almost delight.

In the midst of her wildest paroxysm there came a knocking at the door. She started up, her face positively illuminated.

"They have come back!" she murmured in ecstasy.

She rushed to the door and undid its fastenings with fingers tremulous from eager joy. A neighbor confronted her, staring in dismay and amazement at her strange and dishevelled appearance.

"What's come to ye, Dele?" he demanded roughly, though not unkindly. "When ye goin' to put the box in Widder Pettigrove's grave?"

She confronted him for an instant with a wandering look in her eye, as though she had mercifully been driven mad. Then the tyranny of life and habit reasserted itself.

"I'll come up now, Bill," she said.

And she went back to her graves.

THE END.

www.ingramcontent.com/pod-product-compliance
Lightning Source LLC
Chambersburg PA
CBHW021120270326
41929CB00009B/978